TWAYNE'S
FILMMAKERS SERIES

Frank Beaver, Editor

PETER WEIR

Peter Weir on the set of *The Mosquito Coast* (1986).

PETER WEIR
When Cultures Collide

Marek Haltof

TWAYNE PUBLISHERS
An Imprint of Simon & Schuster Macmillan
New York
PRENTICE HALL INTERNATIONAL
London • Mexico City • New Delhi • Singapore • Sydney • Toronto

Twayne's Filmmakers Series

Peter Weir: When Cultures Collide
Marek Haltof

Copyright © 1996 by Twayne Publishers
All rights reserved. No part of this book may be reproduced or transmitted in any form or by any means, electronic or mechanical, including photocopying, recording, or by any information storage and retrieval system, without permission in writing from the Publisher.

Twayne Publishers
An Imprint of Simon & Schuster Macmillan
1633 Broadway
New York, NY 10019

Library of Congress Cataloging-in-Publication Data
Haltof, Marek.
    Peter Weir : when cultures collide / Marek Haltof.
        p.   cm. — (Twayne's filmmakers series)
    Filmography: p.
    Includes bibliographical references and index.
    ISBN 0-8057-7843-8 (cloth : alk paper). — ISBN 0-8057-9244-9 (paper : alk paper)
    1. Weir, Peter, 1944–   —Criticism and interpretation.
I. Title.   II. Series.
PN1998.3.W44H36   1996
791.43'0233'092—dc20   96-27580
                                                                        CIP

The paper used in this publication meets the minimum requirements of American National Standard for Information Sciences—Permanence of Paper for Printed Library Materials ANSI Z39.48-1984.♾™

10 9 8 7 6 5 4 3 2 1 (hc)
10 9 8 7 6 5 4 3 2 1 (pb)

Printed in the United States of America.

For Alma and Margaret

CONTENTS

FOREWORD

Of all the contemporary arts, the motion picture is particularly timely and diverse as a popular culture enterprise. This lively art form cleverly combines storytelling with photography to achieve what has been a quintessential twentieth-century phenomenon. Individual as well as national and cultural interests have made the medium an unusually varied one for artistic expression and analysis. Films have been exploited for commercial gain, for political purposes, for experimentation, and for self-exploration. The various responses to the motion picture have given rise to different labels for both the fun and the seriousness with which this art form has been received, ranging from "the movies" to "cinema." These labels hint at both the theoretical and sociological parameters of the film medium.

A collective art, the motion picture has nevertheless allowed individual genius to flourish in all its artistic and technical areas: directing, screenwriting, cinematography, acting, editing. The medium also encompasses many genres beyond the narrative film, including documentary, animated, and avant-garde expression. The range and diversity of motion pictures suggest rich opportunities for appreciation and for study.

Twayne's Filmmakers Series examines the full panorama of motion picture history and art. Many studies are auteur-oriented and elucidate the work of individual directors whose ideas and cinematic styles make them the authors of their films. Other studies examine film movements and genres or analyze cinema from a national perspective. The series seeks to illuminate all the many aspects of film for the film student, the scholar, and the general reader.

Frank Beaver

PREFACE

My interest in the cinema of Peter Weir, an Australian filmmaker now working in the United States, began in my native Poland, where I graduated from the University of Silesia. Working as a film critic and teaching cultural studies in my hometown, Cieszyn, I witnessed the emergence of Australian New Wave films, particularly those made by Peter Weir, who in 1975 gained international recognition for his *Picnic at Hanging Rock*. At that time Weir's name was for me synonymous with Australian cinema. Furthermore, my images of Australia were images from his, and other, New Wave films. They created a picture of that country that survived almost unchanged until I arrived in Adelaide, South Australia, in 1986.

While living in Australia, I began work on a master's degree with a relatively narrow topic: the relationship between dream and film in Weir's cinema. By the time I finished my degree, I was not satisfied: I had become aware of the films' cultural context, deeply rooted in Australia's history, and I also saw them as Weir's effort to deal with Australian cultural myths and to elucidate the notion of the Australian nation.

In the early 1980s, after making his name in Australia, Weir moved to the United States, as did a number of Australian filmmakers. Having lived in North America (Canada) myself, I view Weir's American-made films as both a continuation and a development of his Australian interests and cinematic style. I try to look at his recent films through the prism of his early achievements.

My approach to Weir's films draws mostly on the critical concept of *auteurism*. The focus is on the themes, structures, and cinematic devices Weir employs in his films as well as on the cultural and ideological context of his films: intertextuality (literary and filmic), political concerns, and mythologies.

Because this is an *auteur* study, a brief explanation of the term is in order. The French word *auteur* was introduced into the vocabulary of film criticism to emphasize that cinema is an art of individual, personal expression that is comparable with other creative activities.

Promoting certain film directors to the status of "author" meant challenging existing modes of thinking about cinema as a phenomenon purely restricted to the domain of popular culture.

The auteur policy (*la politique des auteurs*) was formulated and developed by the contributors to *Cahiers du Cinéma* at the beginning of the 1950s. Since that time, the individual attributes of a directorial style have attracted increasing attention from film critics and theoreticians. Early auteurism, however, was a method of criticism rather than a theory. The concept of *auteur* as an evaluative tool, though useful, did not deal with analysis of particular films and authors. Auteur methodology called the director of a film the author and looked for stylistic and thematic unity in works to prove authorship.

In the United States, the assertion that the director is the sole creator of the film was first and most ardently adopted by Andrew Sarris, who named it "author theory." Since the beginning of the 1960s, the auteur concept, heavily influenced by structuralism (the so-called *auteur-structuralism* or *cine-structuralism*), has been used by a group of British film critics and theorists: Geoffrey Nowell-Smith, Peter Wollen, Jim Kitses, Alan Lovell, and others. The auteur concept now focuses on structures rather than evaluation. The author, according to Wollen, is no longer a person but the representative of a system of relations among a body of works bearing the same signature, a common denominator linking several films together.

The next stage of author theory, loosely described as the poststructuralist phase, emerged mainly with the development of film semiotics and psychoanalysis along with that of historical materialism influenced by the Althusserian notion of ideology. The film is approached as a textual system. The author is perceived not as a source of meaning but as a term "negotiated" in the process of spectating (reading). Auteurism has essentially dominated film criticism for nearly three decades. Functioning as an interpretive strategy, auteurism in practice governs the way a movie is approached and received.

I analyze films grouped under the name *Peter Weir,* works bearing his name. In film criticism, the name *Weir* assumes a set of critical procedures as well as a set of techniques that indicate his visual style and that have thus come to be designated as his authorial style. I examine Weir as a figure created by his films. Thus, in my approach I am not preoccupied with any kind of biography but with Weir as a figure emerging from films authored by him. I look for and try to define his individual style.

In any auteurist approach it is difficult to avoid romantic criteria, such as the question of intentionality and authorial will. It is almost impossible not to look for authorial consciousness, homogeneity, and evolution, while it is easy to neglect the social context and external forces contributing to the process of filmmaking.

My own use of auteur methodology is concerned with the analysis of structures, themes, and cinematic devices employed by Weir in his works. While I remain cognizant of the important contributions of others involved in film production, the question of the extent to which the director has had full control over his work and the extent to which other contributors have influenced it is not of great importance in my approach. For me, the director's work is a synthetic one that combines various contributions into a structural whole and determines the final form of the film.

Chapter 1 situates Peter Weir and his first short films within the context of the Australian New Wave. The following chapters are primarily concerned with the cultural context of Weir's feature films. Chapter 2, "Weir's Australian Gothic," focuses on his early feature films, starting with two medium-length films, *Michael* (1970) and *Homesdale* (1971). Stylistically as well as thematically, they have many features in common with *The Cars That Ate Paris* (1974) and *The Plumber* (1978). These films belong to the prominent subgenre within Australian cinema known as Australian Gothic. The term refers to a group of films attempting to create a nightmarish, grotesque world that, unlike the majority of Australian films, is set in an urban milieu. The next chapter, "Children in the Bush," discusses Weir's first internationally acclaimed film. *Picnic at Hanging Rock* expresses significant patterns of thought, feeling, and behavior characteristic of Australian society. This film is concerned with exploring the "spirit of Australia" and the clash between alien (British) orders and the spirit of the new (Australian) land. Chapter 4, "Dreamtime and Real Time," deals with *The Last Wave* (1977). This film, sometimes called an anthropological thriller, presents the clash between the Western World of logic and Aboriginal tribal lore, between knowledge and magic, real time and "dreamtime." *The Last Wave* belongs to a comparatively small group of Australian films dealing with the country's native inhabitants.

Chapter 5, "The Quest for Self-Identity," discusses Weir's acclaimed film *Gallipoli* (1981). Weir tries to explain the notion of "the Australian nation" by examining such ideas as "good" Australians versus "bad" foreigners, the myth of innocent Australia, and

the attributes of Australianess versus Britishness. The next chapter deals with the concept of the "mysterious Orient" and the typically Australian concept of doubleness, a result of Australia's colonial heritage and its present-day isolation from the world. "Beyond Shadows: *The Year of Living Dangerously*" deals with Weir's attempt to define the notion of Australianess by presenting Indonesia (Asia) as a missing part of Australia. Chapter 7, "*Witness* in the Amish Land," focuses on the 1985 film *Witness* (1985), the first Weir shot entirely within the American film genre and cultural context. It also centers on paradigmatic cultural clashes: the Amish versus other Americans, archaic versus modern ways of life, country versus city, and so forth.

Chapter 8, "Jungle Utopia," deals with *The Mosquito Coast* (1986), a film about a man driven and ultimately conquered by his perception of the American dream. *The Mosquito Coast* could be taken as the tragedy of a strong personality, a cautionary tale on the myths of individual omnipotence, or a variation on the pioneer narrative. The subsequent chapter, "Carpe Diem: Idealism Versus Realism in *Dead Poets Society*," discusses the classic symbolism employed by Weir in this 1989 film. As in his early films, Weir presents the protagonist, a newcomer from the outside world, with a world of unusual beauty whose conservative norms have long since been established. Confronted by an environment strictly governed by its own principles, the newcomer fails in his attempts to rejuvenate it. Chapter 10, "A Parisian in America," focuses on *Green Card* (1990). This film is not only a comedy of manners but also a variation on another favorite Weir theme, the cultural clash between French and American ways of life. The last analytical chapter, "The Days After," discusses *Fearless* (1993), in which a plane crash is the catalyst for the conflict common to Weir's earlier works and prompts actions impossible under ordinary circumstances.

The concluding chapter, "Peter Weir's Personal Style," discusses the major elements Weir employs to organize his films. Weir is one of the few Australian film directors to have developed a distinctive, personal style. In spite of the fact that he has worked within many genres and with different collaborators in Australia and America, his films are linked stylistically, thematically, and ideologically.

ACKNOWLEDGMENTS

I would like to thank the following persons, who helped me, in one way or another, in writing this book. I am most grateful to Professors Alicja Helman (Jagiellonian University in Cracow, Poland) and Edward Możejko (University of Alberta in Edmonton) for years of professional encouragement and for valuable comments on the early version of the manuscript. I am also grateful for similar comments made by Dr. Neil Rattigan (University of New England in Armidale, Australia).

I am particularly thankful to my friends in the Department of Comparative Literature and Film Studies at the University of Alberta: Dr. Paul Morris, Dr. Bohdan Y. Nebesio, and Dr. Waclaw Osadnik. I would like to acknowledge their encouragement and sup-port. I would also like to thank Dr. Anton K. Kozlovic, who sent me research information and discussed various aspects of Weir's films with me, and Alice Nash, who provided editorial assistance. I also wish to acknowledge India Koopman, an editor for Twayne Publish-ers, who made invaluable comments and suggestions.

Research materials were made available to me by the Flinders University of South Australia and the South Australian Film Corpo-ration. To the Flinders University of South Australia and the Univer-sity of Alberta, I wish to express my appreciation for giving me an opportunity to start and to finish this book, respectively.

The photographs that appear in this volume do so courtesy of the following: Atlantic Releasing Corporation, Associated R&R Films Pty Ltd., François Duhamel, Lam Ping Limited, Merrick Morton, MGM/UA Entertainment Co., Paramount Pictures Corporation, Touchstone Pictures, Warner Bros., and World Northal.

A slightly different version of chapter 5 was published in *Journal of Popular Film and Television* 21, no. 1 (1993): 27–36. Reprinted with permission of the Helen Dwight Reid Educational Foundations. Published by Heldref Publications, 1319 18th Street, N.W., Washing-ton, DC 20036-1802. Copyright 1993.

CHRONOLOGY

1944   Peter Weir born 21 August in Sydney.

1962   Enters the University of Sydney for one year, having completed Vaucluse High School and Scots College.

1963   Works for his father's real estate business.

1965   Travels to England. Has first experiences with camera.

1967   Works as a stagehand for Channel Seven in Sydney. Directing debut with the short comedy *Count Vim's Last Exercise.*

1968   *The Life and Flight of the Rev. Buck Shotte,* a parody of religious cults, accepted for the 1969 Sydney Film Festival (withdrawn by Weir).

1969   Works with the Commonwealth Film Unit (later Film Australia) as a director.

1970   *Michael,* a novella in a three-part production, *Three to Go,* wins the Grand Prix from the Australian Film Institute.

1971–1973   Second Grand Prix for the medium-length *Homesdale.* Travels in Europe on a grant. Makes series of short and documentary films for the Commonwealth Film Unit. Best known are *Incredible Floridas* and *Whatever Happened to Green Valley.*

1974   First feature, *The Cars That Ate Paris.*

1975   *Picnic at Hanging Rock,* an international breakthrough for Weir. It is praised at international film festivals, attains status as a cult film in Europe, and becomes the symbol of Australia's film revival.

1977   *The Last Wave,* Weir's first film released in the United States.

1978   *The Plumber,* a made-for–TV movie is also shown in movie theaters, receives critical acclaim in Australia and America.

1981   The historical drama *Gallipoli,* Weir's first feature to be distributed by a major American studio. This seminal Australian film receives nine Australian Film Awards, including best picture and best director.

1982   *The Year of Living Dangerously,* an adaptation of C. J. Koch's acclaimed novel. Oscar-winning performance by Linda Hunt.

1985   Weir's first American film, *Witness,* receives eight Academy Award nominations, including best picture. William Kelley and Earl W. Wallace win for best screenplay.

1986   *The Mosquito Coast,* based on Paul Theroux novel; neither a critical nor a popular success.

1989   *Dead Poets Society* receives four Academy Award nominations. Tom Schulman wins for best screenplay.

1990   *Green Card.* Weir nominated for an Academy Award for his screenplay.

1993   *Fearless* based on the novel by Rafael Yglesias.

CHAPTER I

Peter Weir and the Australian New Wave Cinema

Peter Weir's name is inseparable from the Australian film renaissance of the 1970s. His 1975 film *Picnic at Hanging Rock* was a turning point in the development of the new cinema in Australia as well as in the establishment of Weir's international reputation. He emerged not only as a competent craftsman but also as an auteur whose personal stamp characterized his endeavors. Furthermore, *Picnic at Hanging Rock* and other films directed by Weir were among the most critically and commercially successful Australian films of the New Wave period.

Weir's career has to be read through the prism of the Australian film revival of the 1970s. He both contributed to and is a product of this period of enormous artistic activity. In many respects, Weir's biography resembles that of his New Wave friends; they share similar generational experiences and a '60s sensibility. They started their careers in the 1960s with short films and moved to mainstream feature filmmaking in the mid-1970s. Like Weir, the majority of these filmmakers—Gillian Armstrong, Bruce Beresford, Phillip Noyce, and Fred Schepisi—now pursue their professional careers in the United States, only periodically returning to their home country.

Peter Weir was born in Sydney on 21 August 1944, a fourth-generation Australian whose ancestors were immigrants from Ireland, England and Scotland. He attended Vaucluse High, Scots College, and the

University of Sydney, where he began the study of arts and law. Weir, who has an aversion to formal education systems (which he finds "industrialized" and damning to individual sensibility), dropped out of the university before finishing his first year and, at the age of nineteen, entered his father's one-man real estate business. In 1965, taking the money he made and following in the footsteps of many other young Australians, Weir visited Europe. On his way to England, on the Greek liner *Patris* heading for Piraeus, he and some friends had the opportunity to produce some shows on a closed-circuit television onboard ship. They were inspired by the then-famous Australian television program *The Mavis Bramston Show* and marked Weir's introduction to filmmaking.

After returning from Europe, Weir decided to pursue a television career. At that time he did not consider a future in filmmaking; he was not a filmgoer, and he possessed no theoretical or practical knowledge of the craft. "I was not exposed to any film culture in my teens," he recalls.[1] Like most other would-be filmmakers of his generation, he knew little of either Australian or European filmmaking, having been brought up on popular Hollywood cinema.

In 1967 Weir joined television Channel Seven in Sydney as a stagehand and started producing amateur revues. With help from his friend actor-writer Grahame Bond and the use of facilities provided by the Channel Seven Social Club, Weir was able to produce his first short film. *Count Vim's Last Exercise* (1967), a fifteen-minute offbeat comedy intended as a phony government propaganda film, was met with considerable interest and allowed Weir to make another film. The following year he made his second short film, a parody of religious cults, *The Life and Flight of the Rev. Buck Shotte,* about an eccentric American preacher and his new religion. The film was accepted for screening at the 1969 Sydney Film Festival, but then withdrawn by Weir in protest of the censor's ban of the Swedish film *I Love, You Love* by Stig Björkman.

After the success of his first two films, Weir was able to direct film clips for the satirical television revue *The Mavis Bramston Show.* In 1969 he joined the Australian Commonwealth Film Unit (ACFU, replaced by Film Australia in 1973) as an assistant cameraman and production assistant. Nominally hired as a director, Weir found himself in the prime training ground for aspiring filmmakers before the establishment of the Australian Film and Television School in 1973. "It was like a school," Weir said in 1984. "It was the university that I had looked for in 1963."[2] Like many of the later well-known New

Wave filmmakers, such as Donald Crombie, Arch Nicholson, and Michael Thornhill, Weir had been given an opportunity to learn the craft of directing, to work with bigger budgets in an atmosphere of considerable artistic freedom.

In 1970 Weir directed the filmic novella *Michael* for the three-part ACFU production *Three to Go,* considered a kind of landmark in Australian filmmaking after years of industry stagnation. The other parts were directed by Brian Hannant and Oliver Howes, also associated with the ACFU. *Michael* was followed by an equally successful medium-length effort, a film titled *Homesdale* (1971), made for the Experimental Film and Television Fund (EFTF). Weir spent the next year on a travel grant in Europe writing scripts for future films and learning his craft on feature film sets in England.

On returning to Australia, Weir continued his work for the ACFU with a series of short films in color designed as teaching aids. The first, *Stirring a Pool*—actually made before his trip to Europe in 1975—is a part of the series *Case Studies in Supervision,* a training film featuring an appearance by Australian star Judy Morris, who was then just starting her career. This six-minute film was followed in 1972 by a group of equally short apprenticeship films, also dealing with executive-personnel relations: *Boat Building, The Billiond Room, The Computer Centre,* and *The Field Day. Australian Colour Diary No. 43: Three Directions in Australian Pop Music,* another film produced by ACFU in 1972, looks at developments in the Australian pop-music scene.

Incredible Floridas (1972) and *Whatever Happened to Green Valley* (1973), both produced by the ACFU's successor, Film Australia, are among Weir's most important documentaries of that time. The former is a twelve-minute study of Australian composer Richard Meale and his work *Incredible Floridas,* an homage to the poet Arthur Rimbaud (the phrase "incredible Floridas" is taken from one of Rimbaud's poems).

Whatever Happened to Green Valley concerns a Housing Commission Estate (Green Valley) twenty-five miles west of Sydney, inhabited by about 30,000 people. Supplied with Film Australia equipment, the residents are invited to film themselves as they go about their daily lives. Weir's documentary contains his grotesque vision of Green Valley (which as a typically unpleasant suburb of Sydney is not green at all), the residents' films, and a final community-based discussion. *Whatever Happened to Green Valley,* scripted and directed and with an appearance by Weir, is an original example of a documentary about a documentary, an experiment in cinema verité.

In 1974 Weir directed his first feature film, *The Cars That Ate Paris,* sponsored by Australian Film Development Corporation (to become the Australian Film Commission [AFC] in 1975). Between the making of *Count Vim's Last Exercise* and the commercial release of his first feature (from 1967 to 1974), Weir learned his craft. His early films, although understandably amateurish, were important first steps toward artistic maturity. They exhibit interests that would become the focus of his later, widely known films. Weir's international career began with his next film, *Picnic at Hanging Rock.*

Weir's filmmaking career was made possible in part by the stimulating atmosphere of the early 1970s in Australia. After years of artistic inertia, the year 1970 ushered in a number of important political decisions that greatly influenced the future shape of the local film industry. With the establishment of the Australian Film Development Corporation and the Experimental Film and Television Fund—and with the later announcement of the establishment of the Australian Film and Television School in Sydney, in 1973—the most interesting period for the Australian film industry had begun. The importance of the film school in Sydney becomes evident in the second phase of the New Wave thanks to films made by its first talented graduates, Gillian Armstrong and Phillip Noyce.

The Australian feature film industry of the 1970s was largely a creation of government policy. Filmmakers and producers relied heavily on funding provided by government institutions, which, particularly in the first phase of the development of national cinema, were generous in sponsoring films with Australian content. Cinema was treated as a "national project"; financial considerations were of secondary importance at that time. There was, however, a price to pay for promoting "Australianess." As David Stratton writes, by 1980 only about 16 percent of locally produced films were profitable, and 49 percent were box-office failures.[3]

The terms *revival* and *renaissance,* frequently applied to the Australian cinema of the 1970s, suggest a rebirth rather than humble beginnings. Feature films had been produced in Australia prior to 1970, although there was little sense of continuity between the promising start at the beginning of the century and the New Australian cinema to come. Weir and his colleagues, predominantly exposed to American cinema, were largely unaware of their filmic heritage. Nevertheless, Australian cinema, which began with the filming of the 1896 Melbourne Cup horse race, has a history essen-

tially as long as cinemas elsewhere and, perhaps in the early years, one as significant. An Australian Salvation Army film, *Soldiers of the Cross* (1900), which was a combination of slides, film, music, and commentary, is sometimes purported to be the first full-length feature in the world. A similar claim is made about Charles Tait's *The Story of the Ned Kelly Gang* (1906), which was probably the longest narrative film to that date in the world.[4] This film originated the distinct Australian genre of the bushranger, films featuring the mythical Ned Kelly and other bandits from the bush. This form was vibrant until its suppression by the New South Wales police in 1912, under the claim that it encouraged antisocial behavior. During World War I, several films promoting the war effort that were popular with local audiences were made with financial assistance from the military. Alfred Rolfe's *The Hero of the Dardanelles* (1915), for example, exploits the Gallipoli campaign, an event of mythical significance for Australians.

After the war, and in spite of the increasing influence of Hollywood, some of the best Australian silent films were made by Franklyn Barrett (*The Breaking of the Drought* [1920] and *The Girl of the Bush* [1921]) and, in particular, by Raymond Longford. Longford, with the participation of his partner, the actress-director Lottie Lyell, created *The Sentimental Bloke* in 1919 and *On Our Selection* in 1920. The former, especially, is deservedly celebrated for its stylistic and technical mastery as well as for its "Australianess": the use of the vernacular, colloquial humor, and the naturalism of the Woolloomooloo (Sydney's working-class area) scenes.

During the late 1920s and the 1930s, with the arrival of sound, the local film industry entered a period of decline. With some notable exceptions—for instance, films made by the McDonagh sisters (*The Cheaters* [1930]), Ken G. Hall (his new version of *On Our Selection* [1932]), and Charles Chauvel (*Forty Thousand Horsemen* [1940] and *The Rats of Tobruk* [1944])—Australia became a cheap location for British, American, and other foreign films wanting an exotic backdrop for exotic stories. There were, however, exceptions in this case as well: the British Ealing Company presence in Australia resulted in one of the most interesting films of that time, *The Overlanders* (1946), by Harry Watt. Watt presents typical bushmen (with famous Australian actor Chips Rafferty in the leading role) chosen to drive a huge herd of cattle overland in an effort to evade the (much-feared at that time) Japanese invasion.

Efforts to revive film production in Australia failed. During the 1950s and 1960s only a few locally financed feature films were com-

pleted, such as John Heyer's *The Back of Beyond* (1954) and Cecil Holmes's trilogy on mateship (comradeship among men), *Three in One* (1956). Between 1962 and 1965 no film was produced in Australia. Tom Fitzgerald (writing under the pen name Tom Weir) commented on this situation in the influential journal *Nation:* "our voices are thin and so weakly articulated as to be barely audible to visitors when they step ashore. The daydreams we get from celluloid are not Australian daydreams."[5]

In 1963 a Senate committee known as the Vincent Committee, named after its chair, Sen. V. S. Vincent, provided several recommendations for the future development of the national cinema. Although ignored by the Liberal government led by Robert Menzies, these proposals later played a significant role in encouraging government intervention in the Australian film industry.

As early as in 1967, the popular success of Michael Powell's *They're a Weird Mob* proved the growing demand for films speaking in a distinct Australian idiom. Independent, personal films such as *Time in Summer* (1968) by Ludwik Dutkiewicz and the better-known *2000 Weeks* (1969) by Tim Burstall, along with films made by independent production companies such as Carlton Cinema in Melbourne and Ubu Films in Sydney, had shown the artistic potential of the local cinema in Australia.

In the late 1960s, government intervention in the film industry started up a new era in Australian cinema. A Labor government headed by John Gorton, and later by Gough Whitlam, shook off the industry's period of relative inactivity. Nearly all the films of the 1970s were made with government money. Together with the state governments, the federal government began investing in film and promoting "culturally worthwhile" films, giving Australia not only recognition but a sense of cultural distinction. In 1973 the first state film company, the South Australian Film Corporation, was established, known for its involvement in such films as *Sunday Too Far Away* (1975) and *Storm Boy* (1976). The corporation also produced Weir's *Picnic at Hanging Rock* and *The Plumber* (1978) and contributed to the production of his *The Last Wave* (1977) and *Gallipoli* (1981).

The reemergence of the national cinema was also due to the increasing interest in cinema in general and in the history of local cinema in particular. This was evidenced by the appearance of the first film programs at universities, the first cinema journals (such as *Cinema Papers,* first published in 1974), and the first book on Australian cinema (John Baxter's *The Australian Cinema,* published in

1970).[6] Apart from that, a strong film lobby pressed the government to establish the legal basis for a national cinema. In a series of articles published in prominent Australian journals, Phillip Adams, Colin Bennett, Sylvia Lawson, Michael Thornhill, and others opted for government intervention and the creation of government bodies responsible for sponsoring the local film industry.

Owing to the government's involvement in film in the 1970s, 153 feature films were made, compared with 5 at the beginning of the century, 163 in the 1910s, 90 in the 1920s, 51 in the 1930s, 19 in the 1940s, 25 in the 1950s, and only 17 in the 1960s. In the 1980s, 335 films were made. These were mostly low-budget films by American standards (costing an average of $300,000–$400,000, which then had about the same value in American and Australian terms), relying on a sympathetic local audience. Between 1970 (the introduction of many government programs) and 1988 (the date of the removal of favorable tax concessions for capital expenditures on filmmaking), about 350 feature films, 150 television movies, and 100 television miniseries were made.[7]

The first Australian films of the 1970s to reach an international audience were foreign productions dealing with Australian mythology. Tony Richardson's abortive attempt to revitalize the bushranger genre, *Ned Kelly* (1970), along with Nicolas Roeg's *Walkabout* and Ted Kotcheff's *Wake in Fright* (U.S. title: *Outback*), both released in 1971, looked at the unique, austere qualities of the Australian landscape and called the world's attention to the reemergence of cinema there.

It is only since 1975 that we can speak of an Australian film renaissance. Ken Hannam's *Sunday Too Far Away* and Peter Weir's *Picnic at Hanging Rock* were released in that year and received significant recognition in Australia and overseas. These two films were followed by a group of distinguished productions, often called "nostalgia" or "history" or AFC films.[8] The best known are Don Crombie's *Caddie* (1976) and *The Irishman* (1978), Bruce Beresford's *The Getting of Wisdom* (1977) and *Breaker Morant* (1980), Fred Schepisi's *The Devil's Playground* (1976) and *The Chant of Jimmie Blacksmith* (1978), Phil Noyce's *Newsfront* (1978), Gillian Armstrong's *My Brilliant Career* (1979), and Weir's *Gallipoli* (1981).

These and other films were not only commercial successes but also became internationally known as the Australian New Wave. Weir's name became virtually synonymous with this period of outburst in creative energy. Looking back at the beginning of his career, Weir

states: "I enjoyed the comfort and the firepower of the studio picture, and I was dealing with amazingly professional people who were also extremely generous in the creative area of leaving it to me."[9]

The emergence of Australian New Wave films coincided with discussions of the national image of Australia. The nationalism presented in these films clearly differs from that projected by a preceding group of works—the "ocker" films, such as Bruce Beresford's *Adventures of Barry McKenzie* (1972) and Tim Burstall's *Alvin Purple* (1973) and *Petersen* (1974). The ocker films celebrated contemporary urban heroes (ockers) with their vernacular, characteristically vulgar behavior and masculine habits. These popular films were made for the Australian market and successfully competed there with Hollywood products. The New Wave films were mostly period films defining nationhood not only through current mythologies and realities but through discourse on the meaning of the Australian nation in the colonial past and during the first years of independence.

Australian films of the 1970s, including Weir's Australian-made films, took part in a "building-a-nation" process, in "inventing Australia," as Richard White puts it in the title of his seminal book.[10] The AFC films reinforced the principal myths of Australian national identity, such as the myth of the bush and its inhabitant, the bushman, the myth of mateship, and the Anzac (Australian and New Zealand Army Corps) legend. The purpose of this endeavor was to create an acceptable image of Australia and to promote it overseas. The mythological was of greater importance here than historical accuracy or truth. As Ina Bertrand bluntly stated in 1984: "Truth is not an issue here. As a nation we can live without 'truth': perhaps we prefer not to know if the truth is unpleasant or, even worse, boring. But we cannot continue to exist without a sense of self, identity, in this case 'Australianness.' "[11]

Of course, it would be incorrect to speak of Australian cinema as a kind of monolith. This was not a single, homogeneous industry but a diverse cinema ranging from Beresford's ocker comedies and Paul Cox's art cinema to George (*Mad Max*) Miller's futuristic nightmares. It is possible, however, to name the dominant trends closely associated with two major influences on Australian cinema: European art cinema and classic Hollywood cinematic style; both influences are discernible in Weir's productions. *Picnic at Hanging Rock,* for instance, was modeled on European art cinema represented by, among others, the Swedish film *Elvira Madigan* (1967) by Bo Widerberg, which enjoyed extreme popularity in Australia. The influence of classic

Hollywood filmmaking is visible in particular in the context of the second stage of the development of modern Australian cinema, mostly in "popular" cinema. The *Mad Max* series, for instance, is an Australian reworking of the Hollywood action narratives found in such popular genres as science fiction, the western, and crime film. Weir's *The Cars That Ate Paris* and *The Year of Living Dangerously*, in particular, although not belonging to any single genre, were also influenced by Hollywood filmmaking.

CHAPTER 2

Weir's Australian Gothic: *Michael, Homesdale, The Cars That Ate Paris, The Plumber*

The terrifying thing in those early films was not knowing why something had worked, even more than understanding why something hadn't worked.
— Peter Weir, quoted in Sue Matthews, *35mm Dreams*

The first success for Peter Weir came with his short film *Michael,* released in 1970, the second part of the trilogy *Three to Go* made by the Commonwealth Film Unit. *Michael,* like the other two films in the series—Brian Hannant's *Judy* and Oliver Howes's *Toula*—was built around the problems of contemporary young Australians. *Michael* won the Grand Prix from the Australian Film Institute in 1970. In their indispensable history of the Australian film industry, Graham Shirley and Brian Adams observe: "Each episode was unique, not only because of strong personal commitment on the part of the directors, but also as government films made by young directors confronting audiences with issues relevant to their generation" (Shirley and Adams, 265). Produced and supervised by Gil Brealey, *Three to Go* was the culmination of the Commonwealth Film Unit's attempts to create a local film industry.

Weir based his project on a script entitled "Rebellion," which he had written and tried to sell for inclusion in the current affairs televi-

sion program *Four Corners.* For the purpose of *Three to Go* he changed his story from one about terrorism and a political kidnapping to one about a conservative young man, Michael, attracted to hippie culture (Shirley and Adams, 265). This partly autobiographical film was originally shot on 16mm and then blown up to 35mm for its cinema release.[1]

The film opens with a newsreel-like scene of guerilla warfare in the streets of Sydney, which later appears to be a part of Michael's dream. Then, the protagonist (Matthew Burton) meets a group of hippies whose leader, played by writer–actor Grahame Bond, attracts him and becomes his new exotic friend and guide to unknown, forbidden realms. Michael, a young man from a wealthy middle-class family, consequently faces a choice between his "oppressive" class and a "permissive" group of radicals who embody freedom and an anti-authoritarian spirit.

The film as a whole resembles a dream, a rather naive and simplistic dream about the possibilities of counterculture in the late 1960s. Viewed in this way, *Michael* can be considered a sensitive mirror reflecting the era of the Beatles and the Vietnam War. Weir declares that the film merely demonstrates his "political naivete and the naivete of the times" (Matthews, 86).

The young rebels in *Michael* are confronted with representatives of the middle class. In retrospect, both groups look almost grotesque: the businessmen in a queue for the bus, all wearing the same suit and reading the *Australian,* are nearly as funny as the hippies' claptrap and slogans about world revolution, freedom, and capitalism. I tend to agree with Brian McFarlane's opinion that in contemporary society, *Michael* looks rather "like a simplistic examination of youthful rebellion and an equally simplistic repudiation of its values."[2]

Instead of dialogue, Weir employs rock music written and performed by the popular group the Cleves. Rock music, some of the lyrics, and fast editing create a 1960s atmosphere and establish the film's distinctive mood. The protagonist's frame of mind is reflected through the use of popular music. In part, however, this heavy reliance on music in *Michael* and the minimal use of dialogue are due to the fact that, as Weir comments, Australians weren't accustomed to hearing their own accent in films, and actors were afraid to use it (Matthews, 87).

In *Michael,* for the first time, two important aspects of Weir's films appear: a distinctive archetypal protagonist and an equally unique sense of humor. As for the former, this is the character interested in

practices of other groups or cultures, an observer who attempts to rationalize strange occurrences around him. A similar protagonist, presented in slightly different versions and contexts, can be detected in all of Weir's later films. *Michael* is by no means an anti–middle-class film, although it was probably intended as such. It is nevertheless a grotesque vision of the late 1960s in which we can detect Weir's peculiar sense of humor and view of Australian society. This sense of humor is also present in his later, more ambitious films, with the exception of the somber *Picnic at Hanging Rock* and *The Last Wave*.

When compared with these later productions, *Michael* lacks mystery. Although humorous and at times engaging, *Michael* precedes a group of more professional works, similar in style, whose common denominator is an attempt to create a disturbing, nightmarish atmosphere. These films, often called black comedies or Australian Gothic, include *Homesdale* (1971), *The Cars That Ate Paris* (1974), and, most absorbing and coherent, *The Plumber* (1978). According to Susan Dermody and Elizabeth Jacka, Weir's *Homesdale* marks the emergence of Australian Gothic, a group of films consisting of, among others, works by Jim Sharman (*Shirley Thompson versus the Aliens* [1973], *Summer of Secrets* [1976], *The Night of the Prowler* [1977]) and George Miller (*Mad Max* [1979], *The Road Warrior* [1981]). The characteristic feature of Australian Gothic is its perpetual reference to popular culture, its eclectic visual style and the persistent use of the grotesque and the perverse, its suburban setting, and the absence of an immediately identifiable Australian landscape (Dermody and Jacka, 49–52),

In these films, parody and grotesque vision play an important part. However, the sense of humor is of a different kind from that in Weir's later productions. In his early films there is black humor, as in Alfred Hitchcock's works. Moreover, in *Homesdale* and *The Plumber,* there are echoes of Hitchcock's *Psycho,* particularly of the famous shower scene. With regard to these similarities Weir comments, "I've seen reviews of my films which have seen them in terms of a black humour, but I don't think that's accurate. I suppose it depends on the way you see things. Maybe bizarre or strange, but I prefer words like enigmatic, curious or fascinating."[3]

In Weir's fifty-two-minute *Homesdale,* tension between the real and the unreal, between the grotesque and the "normal" is created. The plot of the film is typical for Weir: the protagonist, Mr. Malfrey (Geoff Malone), faces a number of inexplicable incidents in a private guesthouse—Homesdale Hunting Lodge—located on a secluded

island. In the first scene, the guests arrive by ferry. The camera captures their faces and shows their diversity. Both the Homesdale staff and the arriving guests are grotesque. Kevin (Grahame Bond), a pop star and former butcher, and timid Mr. Malfrey stand out from the rest. The expectant guesthouse manager (James Dellit) affords the newcomers an opportunity to release the tensions of everyday life. His staff is a collection of bizarre, grotesque figures, including a malevolent gardener, Neville, played by the now-famous director Phil Noyce. An unusual soundtrack of primitive drum music, which resembles Jill Cowper's music from New Guinea in *The Plumber,* accompanies the guests entering Homesdale.

In spite of some Gothic elements (an island, an isolated locale, the demonic staff), Weir's interest does not lie in the exploration of Gothic themes and atmosphere. Instead, he tries to create a mood characteristic of black comedy. In this type of drama, humanity is driven by forces beyond understanding and control. Characters are presented as disillusioned; they act without motives and events occur without cause. All endings are only illusions. The unexpected end to *Homesdale,* when Mr. Malfrey becomes a member of the guesthouse staff after the murder of the singer-butcher Kevin, confirms such a supposition. The singing of "We are the boys of Homesdale" ends the film. The staff of Homesdale, including Mr. Malfrey, awaits new guests.

Homesdale can also be taken as a dark parody of psychotherapy, as demonstrated by the method of portraying the manager of the guesthouse, the preparations for the "treasure hunt" and the hunt itself, and the guests' performances as arranged and commented on by the manager, who promises his patient-guests complete liberation from everyday pressures: "Homesdale will help you—help you to face the truth."

The film can be construed as a kind of nightmare of Mr. Malfrey. The thematic pattern and atmosphere of *Homesdale,* vacillating between parody and horror, confirm that the film is Mr. Malfrey's bad dream: he experiences anxiety and horror but, simultaneously, moments of pleasure and mystery. As in a dream, incidents are disconnected and elements of comedy and horror are inseparably bound. Weir's later films, though more mature and more coherent, employ the same thematic pattern that began with the semiamateurish films *Michael* and *Homesdale.*

In his full-length feature film debut, *The Cars That Ate Paris,*[4] Weir presents the same hero, another isolated community, a similar black

sense of humor and, what later becomes his trademark, the clash of people representing different cultures.

The protagonist of *The Cars That Ate Paris,* Arthur Waldo (Terry Camilleri), finds himself in a situation typical for most of Weir's protagonists. After a car accident near the small Australian country town of Paris, he regains consciousness in the local hospital, where he is told that his brother George has been killed in the accident. As a result of this accident Arthur is forced to stay in Paris—he suffers from driving phobia because he blames himself for his brother's death; he also remembers his first accident, in which an old man was killed and in which he was at fault. Consequently, he is welcomed into the town and into the mayor's (John Meillon) house. The viewer then sees Paris and its strange inhabitants through Arthur's eyes.

The protagonist is forced to deal with mysterious events and horrors beyond rational explanation. Seen as a whole, the film can be taken as the hero's bad dream. *The Cars That Ate Paris* opens with a commercial-like scene, in a style parodying a cigarette advertisement, and ends showing the protagonist's escape from the wrecked town. Trapped, Arthur gradually realizes that the economy of Paris is based on carefully planned road accidents. The victims' cars and belongings are taken as trophies, and their sale is the town's only source of income. The victims themselves are reduced to a zombie-like state in the Bellevue Ward of the local hospital by the mad Dr. Midland (Kevin Miles), who resembles the famous Dr. Frankenstein.

Arthur also observes a confrontation between the older generation of Paris and a gang of the local youths. The town is terrorized by its delinquent younger generation, who ride in bizarre vehicles constructed from the remains of demolished cars. Daryl (Chris Haywood), a hospital orderly, is leading them in their rebellion against the autocratic rules of the mayor. In the film's final sequence, during the masquerade Pioneers' Ball, the youths' vehicles, armed with spikes and grotesquely decorated, charge through the streets of Paris. Eventually, a brutal battle with the older townspeople occurs. Arthur, who is, unfortunately, the parking inspector, has to take sides in this conflict. He chooses to support the sinister mayor. As Arthur destroys one of the cars and fiercely kills its driver, Daryl, he awakens from inertia. He overcomes his fear of driving and, in spite of the warnings of the mayor ("You cannot leave the town. There are no safe roads. The traps are everywhere"), drives off, leaving the demolished town of Paris.

Several critics praised the film and emphasized that *The Cars That Ate Paris,* though not so ambitious as Weir's later works, is more

coherent and deserves critical attention.[5] I do not, however, share this opinion. Compared with the later *The Plumber*, *The Cars That Ate Paris* lacks direction and rigor in narration as well as in style. The film's energy and its macabre sense of humor are weakened by its undisciplined and inconsistent direction.

Stylistic ambiguity permeates the film from its very beginning. The opening, appearing before the credits sequence, shows a young couple driving a sportscar through the countryside. The screen is filled with images usually associated with television advertisements: a beautiful couple enjoying the outdoors, images of picturesque bush landscape, a flock of sheep, Alpine cigarettes, and Coca-Cola. This flow of images beautifying reality is abruptly interrupted by a car accident, and the camera reveals a small country town positioned in a valley.

The commercial-like sequence is followed by a realistic one. After the credits, Arthur Waldo and his brother George are shown traveling in an old camper wagon. Images from this sequence debunk the idealistic tone of the previous sequence: two ordinary looking men in an ordinary car, three men hurriedly loading a kangaroo into the car's trunk, a visit to the local employment office.

Weir plays with a variety of themes, moods, and genres ranging from parody and comedy to the western, science fiction, and horror. This results in a lack of tension in the film. In spite of the accumulation of the iconography of Hollywood westerns (the confrontation between "good guys" and "bad guys" on the main street, intensified by Western music; horses replaced by cars) and elements of science fiction (the mad doctor and his psychotic experiments), *The Cars That Ate Paris* is permeated with a sense of the macabre and fluctuates between horror and black comedy. Further, the music employed in the film is unconvincing. As a rule, music in Weir's films plays an important role in creating a dreamlike atmosphere. Unlike both his earlier and his later works, the music in this film is without a homogeneous style and does not foster a special mood.

Owing to elements connected with the motif of romantic isolation (the small town nestled in the green hills being a deathtrap for outsiders), the film can be regarded as an attempt to create a Gothic horror story. The small town is a black hole of sorts for anyone who dares to go near it. Though it is suggested that the mayor of Paris wishes to adopt a son, the reasons why Arthur has been spared are not clear. He is the only outsider who manages to penetrate the closed community. Another stranger, the enigmatic clergyman Ted

Mulray (Max Phipps), is not privy to the town's mysteries. "One thing close families don't do. They don't talk to outsiders like Ted Mulray," the mayor warns Arthur. Later, the clergyman is murdered.

Making up the most horrifying aspect of the film are the people of Paris. Beneath the surface of everyday behavior there lies horror. Unfortunately, in this film Weir indicates rather than develops: he accumulates strange features for the sake of making the film bizarre. Most of the characters, with the exception of the protagonist and the mayor, have fragmented appearances: the town idiot, Charlie (Bruce Spence), collecting Jaguar mascots; old women sitting in front of their houses and polishing fragments of dismantled cars; the mayor's wife, Beth, wearing a "second-hand" mink coat but only around the house. Still, in spite of these weaknesses, Weir's observation of seemingly ordinary people and their behavior confirms that his main interest lies in penetrating the extraordinary or even supernatural phenomena that exist within ordinary occurrences. Hidden behind the ordinary, there are threatening and nightmarish phenomena. This idea is developed more fully in Weir's later features, in which terrifying, inexplicable incidents disturb a familiar order.

Horror in *The Cars That Ate Paris* is neutralized by Weir's flippant comments (several remarks of the clergyman, such as the one at a funeral: "Gosh, Lord, sometimes Your ways are downright incomprehensible"), and the use of graphic violence. The film's final sequence, a careful balance between horror and comedy, is the best example of absurdist Gothic self-parody, reminiscent of Grand Guignol theater (in its stress on horror) and very much in the spirit of the anti-Hollywood tradition of exploitation "gore" horror established by Herschell Gordon Lewis (*Blood Feast* [1963] and its derivatives). The surreal violence is emphasized in the portrayal of the cars: their appearance is often heralded and accompanied by animal-like noises. In Weir's film, vehicles have lives of their own: the drivers are virtually invisible, hidden behind cars' blades and spikes. In a sense, *The Cars That Ate Paris* heralds George Miller's dark, futuristic *Mad Max* series.

Neil Rattigan looks at this film from a broader perspective. He believes that Paris may be a "metaphor for Australia itself—especially in its insularity, its insistence on community consensus, and its dependence upon the (feared) outside for its economic well-being."[6] While I agree, in principle, with Rattigan's perceptive comment, Weir's film can be viewed in broader terms still as a critique of capitalist, materialist society (car as fetish, people scavenging off of other people). As indicated by its very title, the film works as a metaphor:

Paris could be replaced with another town, could be placed any-where.

Among Weir's Gothic films the most perfectly realized, and one of the most intelligent, is *The Plumber,* a psychological thriller he wrote and directed for the South Australian Film Corporation and Aus-tralian television's Channel Nine. Like *Homesdale,* this film opens with a shower scene, another reference to *Psycho.* With this scene Weir not only creates a nightmarish Hitchcockian atmosphere of a "desperate struggle for sanity and survival"[7] but also introduces an equilibrium between comedy and horror.

  The Plumber examines the clash between an educated woman, Jill Cowper (Judy Morris), preparing her master's thesis in cultural anthropology, and a stranger, a mysterious plumber named Max (Ivar Kants). Ironically, the aspiring anthropologist, a specialist in the cul-ture of tribes of New Guinea, is unable to understand a "primitive" young man from her own culture who violates her privacy and frightens her.

  The whole situation resembles the encounter of the lawyer and the Aboriginal shaman in *The Last Wave* but is more nightmarish and juxtaposes not two cultures (Aborigines/whites) but two different people from the same culture. A scene in the script, which, interest-ingly, appears in a shortened version in the production, is key to understanding this conflict. In her diary from New Guinea, from where she has recently returned, Jill describes her unusual encounter with a shaman who entered her tent and frightened her by perform-ing his rituals. Jill's husband, Brian (Robert Coleby), loudly reads the following fragment from her notes,

> On the night of 23rd April he came to my tent. He was covered in ceremonial paint, the patterns and markings of which were unknown to me. He sat on the tent floor and motioned for me to do likewise. Then began a ceremony which involved the drinking of a pungent juice which induced a kind of trance, and for several hours he shouted at me various ritual words which I did not understand. I knew instinc-tively I must not show fear or attempt to leave. The ceremony contin-ued till near dawn gradually building in intensity—the man becoming physically aroused, and his actions increasingly threatening. In the tent was a bowl of goat's milk. This I seized, and lifted above my head, holding it there for just a moment. Then I hurled the content in his face. The spell was broken. Curiously, the man burst into tears.[8]

Brian, a medical researcher, advises Jill to include this fragment in her thesis. "It could become a best-seller," he says, intrigued with the story but not interested in Jill's mental state. He tries to explain her fear of the stranger away by deemphasizing the danger of the situation ("He is not some sort of monster") and by accusing his wife of having "too much imagination."

The sexual threat Jill experienced in New Guinea recurs. Now the object of her fear is an ambiguous working class man called Max. The viewer empathizes with Jill and her doubts as to whether the plumber is an innocent eccentric or a real threat. He verbally and physically frightens her by talking about his past, especially his having served time for rape. He takes a shower without her permission. She feels increasingly threatened by him.

Throughout the film Jill listens to music recorded in New Guinea; it causes her to be drawn back to her encounter with the shaman. As Marsha Kinder says, it "leads us to see this earlier encounter as the 'germinal seed' that controls Jill's reactions to the plumber and to reinterpret her interaction with Max in this ethnographic context" (Kinder, 19).

Although she specializes in primitive cultures, Jill fails to wholly understand them and fears their rituals. She is not a researcher coolly categorizing phenomena around her. Isolated in her apartment in a huge university high-rise, she fears another "primitive" ritual performed by another "primitive" man. Jill's apartment is scattered with various tribal artifacts gathered during her research in New Guinea ("Museum in here, eh"? remarks Max). The ambiguous plumber invades this closed world and threatens its existence. What is perceived as a threat by Jill is observed differently by others. Jill's neighbor and friend, Meg (Candy Raymond), comments that "it's a turn-on to have a spunky man working around the house." For Brian he is "quite likeable." "Don't listen to a thing," he says. "He is oversexed and overpaid," states the building superintendent's wife.

Max, the mysterious plumber, is frightening but at the same time charming and humorous, fascinating and repulsive. He is also a good observer. He notices Jill's nervousness and restlessness as well as her husband's neglect of her. The ambiguous nature of the plumber is apparent during his first appearance, and Weir maintains this ambiguity throughout the film. We do not know whether the threat of the stranger is a product of the protagonist's imagination or if it is a real menace. Like her husband, Max tells her: "You are a bit on the neurotic side. Too much imagination." These accusations from both her

husband and the plumber prompt her to lose faith in herself and in her perception of reality. "I felt like I was losing control. It had never happened before," she reveals later to Brian.

The occurrence in New Guinea that she describes in her diary becomes a model for her behavior. She is shy, passive, and frightened in the face of potential danger that is not only of a sexual but also of a psychical nature. Pushing her endurance to the very edge, she anticipates being attacked and suddenly turns on her "tormentor" and humiliates him: Jill reprimands the plumber for his poor English grammar, thus belittling him in front of Meg. She also threatens to get him fired. Finally, she puts her new watch, a gift from Brian, and some money, in Max's car and accuses him of stealing; he is sent to prison. Although innocent in this instance, Max is guilty of other offenses, including violation of her privacy; so her act seems justified in part.

The Plumber can be taken as a strong criticism of the sterile lives of intellectuals. The academics are interested in exotic, snobbish issues, while the goings-on around them are beyond their comprehension. Jill's husband is interested only in getting a position with the World Health Organization in Geneva; Jill, working in comparative isolation, is haunted by her work and her New Guinean experience. Weir stands at an ironic distance that reveals their helplessness. Face to face with difficulties in their everyday lives, when their routine is disrupted, they cannot apply the sophisticated methods they found so useful in their analysis of distant primitive tribal habits. There they are able to use a certain routine procedure—although this can also fail (as in Jill's confrontation with the shaman). When they encounter the same problems within their own culture (for instance, the plumber), they appear helpless (like Jill) or try to belittle the problem (like Brian). Furthermore, even the people from the same social group can have difficulty understanding one another (the Cowpers family).

Although Weir often romanticizes "primitive" people, such as the Aborigines in *The Last Wave* and the Amish community in *Witness,* the film can be viewed as a criticism of both condescending attitudes toward lower-class behavior and "primitive" manners. The academic world can be sterile; the inability to understand rituals different from one's own is characteristic not only of the educated classes. Viewed in this way, *The Plumber* might also be considered a criticism of the "primitive" behavior of lower classes, who are unable to respect the "more sophisticated" rituals of other people. Ironically, the most

primitive but effective solution to the problem of the clash between a well-educated woman and a "primitive" man is used by Jill herself.

The music of the film creates an atmosphere of nightmarish mystery and helps to comment on the narrative as well as to introduce new meanings. While writing her thesis, Jill listens to the sounds of primitive drums recorded in New Guinea. It reminds her of the horrifying situation with the shaman and the sexual threat she experienced there. Most important, thanks to the music, she remembers her final victory over the shaman-oppressor, his humiliation, and her feeling of relief. Each of Max's appearances is heralded by the rock music on his radio, a music similar in its "primitivism" to the drums and similar in its impact on Jill. Her bathroom is transformed by the plumber into a jungle of pipes, another place where magic rituals are performed by another shaman, the plumber. There he sings his own song, a mixture of Bob Dylan music and some verbal banalities. Her final triumph, as she watches from the balcony as Max is being arrested in the parking lot, is emphasized by the playing of tribal chants. A freeze-frame of Jill ends the film. In this way her victorious moment of domination over the intruder is prolonged.

The power of the film lies in its questioning of the rituals of both the shaman and Max as "primitive" men and those of the middle class, represented by academics. Rituals create a self-defense system for the user. Anxiety is transferred from a situation to a ritual. People no longer fear the real threat but rather an encroachment on their ritual. *The Plumber* portrays a situation in which people, hidden behind the iron curtain of their rituals, are unable to understand each other. There is a grotesque scene illustrating this helplessness. It occurs during a meeting with representatives of the World Health Organization during which Brian tries to impress his guests, hoping to obtain a recommendation for a prestigious scholarship. Suddenly, when one of the guests has to use the bathroom demolished by Max, civilized rituals are broken. Using a primitive totem, the rest try to enter the locked bathroom and to deliver the scientist imprisoned in the labyrinth of pipes. Ironically, instead of ruining the evening, this incident improves the atmosphere of the meeting and enables Brian to get an invitation to Geneva.

In discussing *The Plumber,* one cannot escape the inevitable comparison with the fictional world of Harold Pinter's plays and screenplays. Marsha Kinder, who with Beverle Houston coauthored an essay about Pinter's collaboration with British filmmaker Joseph Losey,[9] sees Weir's film as a "Pinteresque black comedy" (Kinder, 17).

Many features justify this comparison. *The Plumber* is about a power struggle that involves sexual as well as class struggle. In many respects it serves as a comment on Australian class divisions (which exist in spite of the egalitarian myth of Australia) and gender roles. As in many of Pinter's works, this film introduces a mysterious stranger-invader who violates somebody else's privacy. The routine check-up of plumbing facilities goes absurdly out of control and turns into a desperate struggle for survival. The ordinary is the source of threat. The action takes place in a claustrophobic space that intensifies this mood of menace; the psychology of the characters is obscured, making them complex and ambiguous. Everything becomes a game of manipulation and a struggle for domination.

The Plumber, however, is also very Weir-like in its thematics: disruption of the familiar order, of middle-class security; an unexplained mystery/threat that is the product of everyday reality and that remains unresolved. From this perspective, the fact that the source of fear is the plumber and his work, which uncovers a hidden labyrinth of pipes in the bathroom, can serve as a symbol of the hidden structure within ordinary life that we take for granted but that may "explode" into something frightening. This simple but complex film foretells in many ways Weir's *Green Card* (1990), another comedy of manners, but without Hitchcockian undertones.

The four films analyzed in this chapter share a similar stylistic pattern and nightmarish atmosphere. The protagonist developed in these first films is present in Weir's later works. In the period between the release of *The Cars That Ate Paris* and *The Plumber* Weir made two important features, *Picnic at Hanging Rock* and *The Last Wave,* which established him as an auteur.

Miranda (Anne Lambert) explores unknown territory in *Picnic at Hanging Rock* (1975).

CHAPTER 3

Children in the Bush:
Picnic at Hanging Rock

He reminded himself that he was in Australia now: in Australia, where anything might happen. In England everything had been done before: quite
often by one's own ancestors, over and over again.
—Joan Lindsay, *Picnic at Hanging Rock*

Picnic at Hanging Rock established Peter Weir as a master in creating an
uncanny, dreamlike atmosphere. It was among the most successful
Australian films of the 1970s. Opening in Adelaide on 8 August
1975, it gradually became a symbol of the Australian film revival. It
was shown in several countries (in the United States as late as 1979,
after the success of *The Last Wave*) to critical acclaim mirrored by
box-office triumph. Though originally ignored by the jury of the
1976 Australian Film Institute Awards, *Picnic at Hanging Rock* won the
1977 British Film Institute Award for best cinematography (Russell
Boyd) and many other awards at smaller international film festivals.

   Picnic at Hanging Rock tells the story of a group of schoolgirls from
an elite private school, Appleyard College, who, on St. Valentine's Day
in 1900, take a field trip to Hanging Rock, a sacred Aboriginal
ground located on the edge of the Australian bush. Two of the girls
and their mathematics teacher never return. In spite of the frantic
search and persistent investigation by the police and by the locals, the
Hanging Rock mystery is never resolved. Many questions are raised
in the film, but no explanation is given.

The script, written by Cliff Green, is based on Joan Lindsay's novel *Picnic at Hanging Rock*, published for the first time in 1967, then by Penguin in 1970, and then reprinted many times following the appearance of Weir's acclaimed film.[1] Unlike the film, Lindsay's work is a nostalgic, Victorian melodrama. In fact, this work resembles nineteenth century writing and is aesthetically exceeded by Weir's acclaimed adaptation, which serves as a rare example of the instance in which a film distinctly overshadows its literary source. Not only does the novel almost entirely owe its fame to Weir's film, but it is "read" through the film and interpreted in the same way.

Both Lindsay's novel and Weir's adaptation echo the way in which British encounters with an alien, Australian land have been presented in various Australian forms of artistic expression. The major theme is the European (British) intrusion into an unfamiliar environment. The intruders are either rejected or defeated. *Picnic at Hanging Rock* shows the incompatibility of British and Australian orders. Desperate and unsuccessful attempts to preserve old orders in alien circumstances and to impose them onto the new land end in disaster.

There is a conscious attempt in the novel to convince the reader to believe that the events at Hanging Rock really happened. At the beginning Lindsay points out, "Whether *Picnic at Hanging Rock* is fact or fiction, my readers must decide for themselves. As the fateful picnic took place in the year nineteen hundred, and all the characters who appear in this book are long since dead, it hardly seems important" (6). This introductory statement and other comments by Lindsay (an excerpt from a Melbourne newspaper, letters, picnickers' testimonies, police reports) try to maintain the balance between fact and fiction. However, like the film, the novel describes events hovering between the realistic and unrealistic, between dream and reality.

I am in agreement with Brian McFarlane that Lindsay's novel is "banal," "pretentious," "snobbish" and owes its fame to Weir's film.[2] The "snobbery" in Lindsay's narrative is seen by McFarlane not only in its sentimental narration but primarily in the patronizing treatment of the lower classes; for instance, their vulgar manners are contrasted with the sophisticated manners of the upper, English classes. Many passages in Lindsay's work support McFarlane's assertion. Lindsay not only differentiates between the sexual conventions of the upper and the lower classes, but also presents a contrast in their behavior. Colonel Fitzhubert's family still cultivates Victorian values and ways of dressing. Formal dresses in the bush, including top hats, corsets, parasols, and other accessories, belong to the old order, which

is incompatible with the order of the new land. The lower classes are usually presented as "the children of the new land," more casual in the way they dress and behave. This way of presenting the two classes goes back to nineteenth-century Australian history.[3]

Questions raised or signalled by Lindsay were taken up by Weir in his adaptation of the novel. The film *Picnic at Hanging Rock* is constructed around the following vivid contrasts:

> Culture (civilization) versus Nature (Earth spirit)
> Familiar versus mysterious
> British (old land) versus Australian (Terra incognita)
> Appleyard College versus Hanging Rock
> Upper classes versus lower classes
> (British-Aristocratic) versus (Australian-Democratic)

As does Lindsay, Weir builds his film around the contrasts of two monoliths, Hanging Rock and Appleyard College. The film opens with a shot of an early morning scene at Hanging Rock, which towers over the surrounding landscape. From this scene a dissolve takes the viewer to Appleyard College. The awe-inspiring Rock is photographed like an old Gothic castle; as in Gothic novels or in horror films, it dominates the region and awaits its new victims. The college, and its austere headmistress, Mrs. Appleyard (Rachel Roberts), are portrayed similarly by way of a great number of low- and high-angle shots, which stress the authoritarian character and Victorian repressiveness of the school and its head.

While following the incidents and the characters in the novel closely, Weir's film concentrates on establishing an atmosphere of mystery, abandoning any attempt to reconcile the story with reality. The director traces the effects of the mystery on the people involved and the gradual decline of Mrs. Appleyard and her college without providing any explanation.

In *Picnic at Hanging Rock*, as well as in his other films, Weir shows the limitations of the protagonists' (and, simultaneously, our) knowledge, which fails to answer basic questions. This concept is explicitly addressed in a scene showing a small plant that closes in on itself when touched. The college gardener, Mr. Whitehead, explains to his assistant: "Some questions got answers and some haven't." Some phenomena are simply beyond comprehension. The more closely we try to observe them and understand them, the more hidden and mysterious they become. Taking this into account, it is not surprising that in

its narrative, characters, and iconography, this film avoids analyses of social and cultural issues in favor of creating dreamlike illusions and a menacing spirit of mystery. Weir's film is more an oneiric enigma than a post-Victorian attempt to deal with the new land.

Picnic at Hanging Rock presents Weir's method of creating a dreamlike atmosphere from the opening shot. The following statement opens the film and appears before the credits: "On Saturday, 14 February 1900, a party of schoolgirls from Appleyard College picnicked at Hanging Rock near Mt. Macedon in the state of Victoria. During the after-noon, several members of the party disappeared without trace. . . ."

This statement nearly explains the whole plot. The film, however, does more than recount incidents that took place on St. Valentine's Day in 1900 in an exclusive country boarding school: mystery and the experience of mystery are explored. The whispered voiceover of a line from a poem by Edgar Allan Poe, "What we see and what we seem, are but a dream. A dream within a dream," spoken by Miranda, one of the schoolgirls, and followed by Gheorghe Zamphir's panpipe music, is a more telling introduction to the film. Unlike the novel, the film is dreamlike, mysterious, and filled with implications. The book presents a more ironic view of the events, but, like the film, the novel ends as it began—an unsolved mystery.

The fatal picnic takes place in an environment described by, among others, one of the first Australian poets, Charles Harpur:

> Not a sound disturbs the air,
> There is quiet everywhere;
> Over plains and over woods
> What a mighty stillness broods.
>
> All the birds and insects keep
> Where the coolest shadows sleep . . .[4]

Before leaving to go on a picnic, Miranda (Anne Lambert) warns the orphan Sara (Margaret Nelson) that she must learn to love others, and mysteriously intimates that she may not return. Then, under the Rock, each person's watch stops at noon. Miss McCraw (Vivean Gray), the mathematics instructor accompanying the girls, tries to explain this phenomenon in rational terms, suggesting that this uncanny event is caused by magnetic emanations from the Rock.

This is the beginning of the supernatural, mysterious events that occur on the Rock. The four girls, led by Miranda, remove black

stockings and boots and head toward the Rock's peak. Then the girls wander through the bush, go to sleep, only to awaken in a trance and begin their exploration of Hanging Rock. The youngest of the girls, corpulent Edith (Christine Schuler), returns inexplicably terrified and, as later revealed, passes by the partially undressed teacher, Miss McCraw. Three girls and their mathematics instructor disappear without a trace. There is no explanation for the disappearance of the girls or for the later discovery of the unconscious but unharmed Irma (Karen Robson), who is unable (or does not want) to tell the truth.

Picnic at Hanging Rock takes place at the beginning of the century, one year before the proclamation of an independent Australia (1901). Thus, it is also a film about the end of the "old world," and the disintegration of Victorian society. Both Appleyard College and Hanging Rock are shown as wonders in the Australian bush. The Rock represents the new land: mysterious, untamed, wild, dangerous, yet fascinating. To use the terminology of Rudolf Otto, a Protestant theologian and philosopher, it serves as a good example of *misterium tremendum et fascinosum* (frightening, yet fascinating experience).[5] The college, however, is totally out of place in Australia, an incongruent remnant of the Empire. Appleyard College is an embodiment of the old world, "an architectural anachronism in the Australian bush—a hopeless misfit in time and space," as Lindsay writes (8). In addition, the college is "quite famed for its discipline, deportment and mastery of English literature" (13). Although for Lindsay the point of reference is perpetually Great Britain, she, like Weir, shows that Appleyard School is a violation of the laws of the new land.

The clash between the two cultures (classes) is demonstrated in the film *Picnic at Hanging Rock* in the relationship of Michael Fitzhubert (Dominic Guard), the young Englishman, and Albert Crundall (John Jarratt), Fitzhubert's Australian coachman. As the girls cross the stream during their ascent to the Rock, they are observed by Michael, who has just recently arrived from England, and by Albert, who comments on Miranda's physical appearance ("She's have a decent pair of legs, all the way to her bum"). He is reprimanded by Michael ("I'd rather you didn't say crude things like that") and responds: "I say the crude things, you just think them." Later, while trying to rescue Irma, Michael collapses on the Rock from exposure. Albert not only saves him but also finds the girl. Glen Levis makes an interesting comment regarding this scene. He believes it symbolizes

the idea of the English having the courage to settle Australia but only native-born white Australians having the ability to deal with the new continent effectively.[6]

The cross-cultural, cross-class relationship between Michael and Albert, however, shows British manners and morals as superior to those of Australians. This treatment is atypical for Australian New Wave cinema and for indigenous Australian literature, in which the British are often ridiculed by the "rough but honest" native-born Australians. In speaking about archetypes of English gentlemen and native Australian bushmen turned Anzacs in the trenches of the 1915 Gallipoli campaign, Geoffrey Dutton shows the persistence in Australian literature of the myth of the wise native Australian who can outperform his educated British counterpart. Dutton comments ironically, "It was a reassuring win for all honest followers of ignorance, laziness and inverted snobbery; it was also a perfectly reasonable act of revenge."[7]

Weir's film stresses a strong thematic concern with the repressed sexuality of the pubescent girls. David Myers explicitly points out that this film is a voyeuristic male fantasy in which young females are portrayed as passive objects of admiration. He declares that "Weir has escaped from a vulgar present to take us on a male voyeur's nostalgia-trip to a sexual utopia for neo-Victorian necrophiliacs."[8] In his review of *Picnic at Hanging Rock*, Richard Combs calls the film a "sexual odyssey,"[9] and this motif appears in critiques. For Brian McFarlane, for instance, the film is a "lushly poetic study of suppressed and burgeoning sexuality" (McFarlane 1980, 12). Weir does not reject this point of view, but for him it is a part of a much bigger theme—nature. "The grand theme was Nature," Weir says, "and even the girls' sexuality was as much a part of that as the lizard crawling across the top of the rock. They were part of the same whole; part of larger questions" (McFarlane and Ryan, 325).

Weir's comment notwithstanding, this film can be seen as a "sexual oneiric odyssey." *Picnic at Hanging Rock* carefully creates an atmosphere of sexual repression; its visual images and the narrative line easily accommodate such an interpretation.

The opening sequence on St. Valentine's morning at Mrs. Appleyard's college shows young, innocent Victorian girls wearing virginal dresses, preparing themselves for a picnic at a place with a strange volcanic formation, Hanging Rock. Russell Boyd's camera captures their excitement and their affected behavior. The girls lace up each

other's corsets, they exchange greetings and glances, play cards, and recite poems. One of the girls imprisons a rose in a flower press. The link between the covert glances, the symbolic, preserved rose, and the pubescent girls is emphasized as they struggle into corsets in their final preparations for the trip.

The girls do not want to listen to Mrs. Appleyard's warning about the dangers of the Rock. "Waiting a million years just for us," says one of the girls during the ride to Hanging Rock. It suggests that the Rock is their destination. Because of its sexual connotations (phallic peaks and vaginal caves), Hanging Rock can also be taken as an emblem of human sexuality. In broader terms, Hanging Rock represents the untamed forces of nature. It is a symbol of ancient knowledge, in this context comparable with Aboriginal dreamtime of *The Last Wave* and the Egyptian pyramids of *Gallipoli*. Mrs. Appleyard, shown in a low-angle shot that enhances the feeling of dominance and oppressiveness, informs the girls that they can remove their gloves in the bush. Further, she warns them that "the Rock is extremely dangerous" and forbids the girls any "tomboy foolishness

Schoolgirls from the elite Appleyard College lace each other's corsets in *Picnic at Hanging Rock* (1975).

in the matter of exploration" of an area well-known for its "ven-
omous snakes and poisonous ants of various species."

Sexual motifs are carefully placed in the narrative. After examining
Edith and Irma the physician repeats that they are "quite intact."
Irma, apart from suffering from shock and exposure, has only
scratches on her hands and head, but her body is mysteriously
unmarked and unblemished. Mrs. Appleyard is convinced that she
understands the mystery. In the end, when she talks with Mlle.
Dianne de Poitiers (Helen Morse) about her dependence on Miss
McCraw, she mentions the suspected rape: "I came to depend so
much on Greta McCraw. So much masculine intellect. I came to rely
on that woman. Trust her. How could she allow herself to be spirited
away? Lost. Raped, murdered in cold blood like a silly schoolgirl."
After Irma (but not her corset) is found, Mrs. Appleyard remarks that
it is even worse that only one of the girls has been found.

Picnic at Hanging Rock contains a series of superimposed shots of
Miranda and a white swan, similar to Leda and the swan in Greek
mythology. Miranda and the swan appear in Michael's mind and in
his dreams: this pairing increases the sexual meanings in the film.
When Michael is asked by Sergeant Bumpher about his thoughts
while observing the girls at the picnic area he does not respond. His
image dissolves into a close-up of Miranda and, then, into an image
of a swan. The same combination of images is repeated later in the
film.

Miranda, a delicate, inspired person, functions as the embodiment
of the pubescent Victorian spirit. She does not even wear her dia-
mond watch because she "cannot stand it ticking above [her] heart."
At the rock she is absorbed by the primal bush. Miranda's image is
also superimposed with the Rock and the image of a flock of birds.
When she opens the gate to the picnic ground, a flock of birds rises
from the ground and frightens the horses. In another memorable
scene, at the picnic ground, Miranda is seen cutting a Valentine cake
with a big knife. Behind her, shown in an extreme low-angle shot, is
the threatening presence of her destination—the Rock.

The use of sexual motifs is best seen in the scene in which Irma,
announced by the French instructor, Mlle. de Poitiers, visits the
school "Temple of Gymnastics" to say goodbye to her friends. Irma is
no longer the girl they once knew. After her experience at Hanging
Rock she has changed from an innocent girl into a mature woman.
Her appearance provokes an almost hysterical reaction from the rest
of the girls. They want to know the whole truth and cry: "Tell us!"

Dressed in scarlet clothes and surrounded by her former schoolmates in white dresses, Irma remains silent.

The story also contains many ambiguous, homoerotic relationships: between Miranda and the persecuted Sara and between Mlle. de Poitiers and Miranda, among others. In his provocative and dissenting review of the film, Ian Hunter addresses the question of lesbianism in *Picnic at Hanging Rock*. He points out the Victoriana in Weir's film and notices that its suggested lesbianism serves as "an emblem of the girls' other-worldliness," a quality drawn from Victorian art, for example, from Coleridge's "Christabel," or Rossetti's "The Bower Meadow."[10]

Picnic at Hanging Rock belongs to the Australian "period/nostalgia" films, which, though perceived as "distinctively Australian," reflected European influences in deferring to European standards of cinematic taste. The "AFC (Australian Film Commission) genre," a term coined by Susan Dermody and Elizabeth Jacka to describe Australian period/nostalgia films, was not prevalent in the 1970s and 1980s, but it was important. The "Australian look" of these films helped to put Australia "on the map."[11] The "Australianess" of the "AFC films" was "constructed" through landscape and history. Dermody and Jacka claim that this is a "national style" determined by the preferences of the funding bodies and hailed critically as a source of national pride. They emphasize this genre's "literariness" (mostly adaptations based on characters rather than action), its "safe nature,"[12] and romantic mise-en-scène. Dermody and Jacka describe the dominant cinematic style of the AFC genre in the following way:

> The approach of the camera is functional rather than expressive. The closest thing to mise-en-scène are lyrical pans across picturesque landscapes or beautifully dressed interiors, giving brief, rapturous play to cinematography's recognition of what is our own. This includes not only distinctly beautiful places, but space, history and cultural traditions. . . . Audiences were to be wooed, reassured, invited to a safe place where no demands would be made beyond feeling with the character, and feeling proudly at home in the setting. Similarly, editing is generally subjugated to a gently paced television-drama notion of the functional, with few passages of action. (34)

Dermody and Jacka, who are critical of this genre's superficiality in describing the local history, see it as the Australian contender for the

"art" film, demonstrating "the sign of 'art' rather than of hard intellectual work" (70).[13]

In many ways *Picnic at Hanging Rock* confirms Dermody and Jacka's assumptions. This film, as well as its literary source, draws on the long tradition of symbolism in art and religion, and especially on dream symbolism. Donald Barrett argues that Lindsay's novel is penetrated by themes that recall the mythology of Pan as presented in classical literature.[14] Recurrent motifs of sleep, dreams, nightmares, and the ever-presence of sexual tension in the novel support this claim. Barrett's point is particularly taken with regard to Weir's film, which not only evokes a dreamlike atmosphere but also plays on mythological themes.

The motif of Pan in the Australian bush was frequent at the turn of the century in Australian painting and writing. Usually, this motif was employed to emphasize the new land's energy, strength, and primitive impulses. The pastoral earth god appeared, among others, in Sydney Long's paintings (*By Tranquil Waters* [1894], *The Spirit of the Plains*, [1897], and *Pan* [1898]), where it served to display the uniqueness of the new continent, and in Norman Lindsay's paintings when inhabited by satyrs, fauns, and other mythic figures (as in *The Picnic God* [1907]).

In her study, "Artemis in South Australia," Karelisa V. Hartigan describes those themes from the cultural representations of ancient Greece which are present in *Picnic at Hanging Rock*. The atmosphere at Appleyard College itself, with all its Victorian character, is totally out of place in the Australian bush country. Moreover, claims Hartigan, the relationship between the headmistress, Mrs. Appleyard, and her girls is different from that at Lesbos: rather, Mrs. Appleyard takes on a sinister resemblance to the vengeful goddess Artemis.[15] Ann Crittenden discusses the film in a similar manner. Apart from looking for mythological and religious significance, her interpretation emphasizes the role of Neoplatonism in building the pattern of events and imagery in *Picnic at Hanging Rock*.[16]

In 1875 William Ford painted his *Picnic Party at Hanging Rock near Macedon*, which hung in the office of Lindsay's husband, Daryl, the director of the National Gallery in Victoria.[17] Before Ford, landscape painters usually stressed the vastness, the strangeness, and the loneliness of the new continent. Ford was the first to see in the bush an idyllic, parklike setting in which well-dressed, prosperous families could spend their leisure time. A second influence on Joan Lindsay was Frederick McCubbin's *The Lost Child* (1886), a painting based on the true story of Clara Crosby, a young girl who survived after

being lost in the bush for three weeks in 1885. Similar influences, one can presume, shaped Weir's film.

It is useful at this point to consider various other factors that may have influenced *Picnic at Hanging Rock*. It should be emphasized that this film was inspired by the Heidelberg School of Australian impressionist painting (Heidelberg is a suburb of Melbourne) and by the Pre-Raphaelites. The Heidelberg School was a distinctive Australian school of painting that between 1885 and 1890 attempted to bring the European way of painting to Australia. This school was the first to interpret the Australian sunlit landscape in a naturalistic manner. This approach contrasted with that of earlier colonial painters, who were interested mostly in stereotypical versions of the Australian topography and in the portrayal of its inhabitants. Opposition to Victorian values was frequently expressed in painting by stressing the harsh beauty of the new landscape and by looking for its distinctive spirit.

The portrayal of the girls in Weir's film resembles depictions from the Pre-Raphaelite paintings, which reflect the Neoplatonic interpretation of nature. Sleeping beauties from Edward Burne-Jones's paintings (*The Rose Bower, The Garden Court*), figures from the portraits by Dante Gabriel Rossetti (*The Day Dream*), Arthur Hughes (*Ophelia*), John Everett Millais (*The Blind Girl*), and others populate the impressionistic Australian landscape in *Picnic at Hanging Rock*.

Apart from Greek mythology, the most frequently cited literary influences are E. M. Forster's *A Passage to India* and Nathaniel Hawthorne's *The Scarlet Letter*.[18] Joan Kirby states that the book and the movie portray the British attempt to combat and control unfamiliar lands (India, America, and Australia) that in spirit and in law resist alien orders. The spirits of the American wilderness, the Australian bush, and the Indian "oriental" landscape are violated by the attempt to subordinate them to an inappropriate, imported order from the Old World.

Weir, following Lindsay, employs the narrative device frequently used in Australian fiction of placing innocent, defenseless characters (mostly children) in an alien environment. John Scheckter points out that the story of the child lost in the bush is sometimes called an "indigenous Australian myth."[19] Scheckter notices that this motif appears for the first time in Henry Kingsley's *The Recollections of Geoffry Hamlyn*, published in 1859, and has since been repeated many times over and has survived almost unchanged.

Though *Picnic at Hanging Rock* seems to be unique in its narrative strategy, it resembles Michelangelo Antonioni's films, particularly

L'avventura (1959), in its lack of final resolution. Antonioni's film also deals with the mysterious disappearance of a young woman, Anna, and the search for her by her lover and her best friend. Like Antonioni, Weir does not permit the viewer to resolve the mystery. *L'avventura*, however, is more preoccupied with the searchers and, similarly, the searchers are more preoccupied with themselves than with the fate of the missing person.

Picnic at Hanging Rock expresses significant social patterns characteristic of Australian society. Australia, one of the most urbanized countries in the world, has a predominantly rural literature. In colonial fiction, the bush was often presented as a background for novels such as those written by Ada Cambridge and Rosa Campbell Praed. Later, Henry Lawson, A. "Banjo" Paterson, and other bush balladists gave graphic accounts of bush life. Lindsay's novel, although written more than sixty years after the publication of Lawson's best works, is a peculiar conglomerate of Victorian values, the ancient belief in an earth spirit, and Aboriginal "dreamtime" ideas. The British intrusion into a hostile land is presented in terms of a nature/culture clash.

Weir's film is also concerned with exploring Australia's physical environment. *Picnic at Hanging Rock* presents humankind's total helplessness when confronted with the inexplicable. On the one hand, nature is too complex to be defined in scientific terms, and on the other, the Aboriginal tracker, who is seen as a part of this nature, is also unable to discover anything more about the incidents on the Rock. The picnic becomes a confrontation with nature, a violation of the "spirit of Australia."

The "spirit of Australia" is presented at its best through the use of the Australian landscape, which is remote from European experiences. The tradition of incorporating the local landscape into Australian films has been widespread. The semantic function of the rural Australian (bush or desert) landscape has always been to delineate the difference between British and Australian. This has perpetually been a part of a larger discourse—the discourse on the Australian national identity.

The centrality of the landscape and its presentation as the site of unknowable terror for white colonists is seen in many genres of contemporary Australian cinema: in "postapocalypse" science fiction (the *Mad Max* series, starting in 1979), "period" or "nostalgia" films (*Burke and Wills* [1985]), horror films (*Long Weekend* [1978]), feminist rewritings of history (*Journey among Women* [1977]), child-centered films

(*Storm Boy* [1976]), and many others. These films are in fact about the Australian landscape: this is their obsession, their leitmotif and central character.

The international success of *Picnic at Hanging Rock* and contemporary Australian cinema is largely due to the fact that it employs and promotes a rural landscape of "exotic" appeal. This was also a factor that brought many foreign (mostly American and British) filmmakers to Australia before the New Wave period. Films made in 1971 by Nicolas Roeg (*Walkabout*) and Ted Kotcheff (*Wake in Fright*) looked to the harsh realities of the Australian interior landscape. Both films used the landscape as the main factor contributing to the creation of an uneasy atmosphere. Although both failed badly at the local box-office, they had a great influence on local filmmaking.

Picnic at Hanging Rock is replete with dream images. To create an atmosphere of mystery, Weir employs many cinematic devices, such as freeze-frames, soft focus, slow motion, and voice-over narration. Furthermore, the plot is not developed in an overly complex fashion; it remains unresolved, and there are dreamlike elements contained in the narrative. The characters have their own dreams; for example, only in a dream can Albert see the sister he has not encountered since their stay in an orphanage, while Michael has visions of Miranda. Unlike other Weir films, with the single exception of *The Last Wave*, *Picnic at Hanging Rock* is a solemn, humorless attempt to create apprehension by employing supernatural events and mysterious occurrences. Because of their unusual, Gothic-like atmosphere, *Picnic at Hanging Rock* and *The Last Wave* have been classified by some critics as horror films.[20] However, too many elements in these films defy this type of interpretation. As opposed to standard horror films, nightmares are not the essence in *Picnic at Hanging Rock* and *The Last Wave;* rather, unknown terrains, inexplicable events, dream, and myth create a feeling of unsettling expectation.

Russell Boyd's cinematography creates hallucinatory compositions and bears a resemblance to great Impressionist painting. Dream images are intensified mainly by employing slow-motion sequences, freeze-frames, and soft-focus shots: Miranda "flows" across the creek, the four girls are shown in slow-motion scenes as they ascend the rock, and a freeze-frame of Miranda ends the film. Soft-focus photography catches the whiteness of the girls' dresses and contrasts it with the color of the rock. When the terrified Edith returns, a high-angle shot shows the rest of the party in a frozen, painterly arrange-

ment. It bears mention that while the film employs many visual stereotypes (such as the virginal image of the girls) and trivialized cinematic devices (slow motion and so forth), it is not hackneyed because such devices purposely serve to transfer the girls from a realistic dimension to a mythical one.

The enigmatic and inspired, but occasionally banal expressions used by the girls, such as Miranda's "everything begins and ends at exactly the right time and place," also create a hallucinatory, oneiric atmosphere. Hunter, in his review of the film, writes: "Landscape doesn't embody time and place—but myth." For him, the mythic, only superficially (because filled with Pre-Raphaelite "nonsense") Australian landscape is the "pictorial incarnation of that notorious Victorian malady, 'the vapors' " (Hunter, 11). Preoccupied with the question of Australianess, Hunter cannot accept a work of art lacking in Australian spirit. He cannot accept that everything in the film is geared toward atmosphere.

Weir emphasizes that the most important aspect of the film, more so than the development of characters, is the creation of a "hallucinatory, mesmeric rhythm."[21] He achieves this result not only through extraordinary camerawork but also thanks to an unusual soundtrack. He often uses eerie silence; the absence of sound enhances the sense of mystery and apprehension. In the first scene, in which the Rock is introduced, Weir employs only natural sounds from the bush (that of insects and birds) with extensive postproduction editing (magnification, speed changes, filtering), obtaining in this way a sense of the supernatural from a natural setting. Similarly, in *The Last Wave*, sounds of torrential rains, working windshield wipers, flowing waters, and so forth are always present. In the early scenes of both films a supernatural mood is established through haunting visual images, specific sounds, and, frequently, blocks of silence.

The atmosphere of *Picnic at Hanging Rock*, as mentioned earlier, is heightened by the mesmeric use of Gheorghe Zamphir's panpipe music, which, perhaps coincidentally, resembles the mood of Count Dracula horror films, set in the Carpathian mountains. In this light, the use of panpipes, as the camera scans the rock, adds new implications to the film. Panpipe music is contrasted with the music of Beethoven's Fifth Piano Concerto in E-flat, opus 73 (the "Emperor" concerto); the visual opposition of nature/culture (Hanging Rock/ Appleyard College) has its sound equivalent in Zamphir's "primitive" music and Beethoven's sophisticated score. A similar contrast between the European culture and a harsh Australian landscape is

achieved during a garden party scene. A string quartet plays Mozart's "Eine Kleine Nachtmusik" while the formally dressed guests try to behave in a way incompatible with the laws of the new land. The camera pans across the party guests and the well-maintained fragment of lawn only to reveal that the place of the party is surrounded by bush.

Color plays a meaningful role in *Picnic at Hanging Rock*. The first part of the film contains mainly impressionistic images: the sun and pastel colors (yellow and green hues, white) dominate the frame. In the second part darker tones appear more frequently (mainly red and brown, as in the headmistress's dark dresses and her shadowy, claustrophobic room), corresponding to Mrs. Appleyard's madness and, subsequently, her death.

There are many unresolved incidents in the film and many characters filled with many layers of meaning. As in other Weir films, there are more questions than answers: questions connected with the disappearance of the girls and Miss McCraw; the Sara/Albert relationship; and Sara's persecution by Mrs. Appleyard, resulting in her suicide. Weir intentionally leaves these and other questions unanswered, mysterious.

In the film's final sequence a voice-over commentary provides information about the fate of Mrs. Appleyard. Her body is found at the base of Hanging Rock, and it is believed that she fell while attempting to climb it. The same voice informs us that the search for the missing girls and their governess continued for the next few years without success and that their disappearance remains a mystery. These last words are accompanied by an extreme slow-motion evocation of the picnic scene under the Rock. Miranda is shown waving goodbye, and the freeze-frame of her turning her head away from the camera ends the film. The shot fades out, leaving the viewer intrigued, bewildered, mystified.

CHAPTER 4

Dreamtime and Real Time in *The Last Wave*

We have lost our dreams. And they come back, and we don't know what they mean.

—David Burton in *The Last Wave*

You are in trouble. You don't know what dreams are any more.

—Chris Lee in *The Last Wave*

As a rule, Peter Weir's films, in particular *Picnic at Hanging Rock* and, later, *Witness,* are characterized by evocative openings. Likewise, *The Last Wave* (1977) opens in silence with a series of highly effective visual shots. The viewer first observes an Aboriginal sand painter in the desert who is working on mysterious signs on a cave wall. In the next scene a group of Aborigines prepare themselves to take shelter, though the sky is cloudless; only the sounds of an imminent storm suggest the change of weather. Then the film cuts to a small country town in the Australian outback tormented by unanticipated torrential rain. From this moment onward, these two elements, the Aborigines and their mythical beliefs linked with unusual, damaging weather conditions, dominate the film.

The Last Wave, Weir's first film to be released in the United States, shares nearly the same narrative pattern as *Picnic at Hanging Rock.* As

in his earlier films, Weir does not focus on empirical observation but on the psychological and anthropological dimensions of his subject.

The first part of the film serves as an example of Weir's cinematic style at its best. From the very beginning, *The Last Wave* consistently establishes the pervasive presence of the supernatural through a chain of climatic disruptions. A remote country town experiences an unprecedented hailstorm, "the first ever recorded fall of hail in the region," as the radio announces later. Big stones of ice fall from the cloudless sky, frightening schoolchildren and their teacher, who remarks that they "are experiencing nature at work." Despite its opening in a remote rural area, the film is set in contemporary Sydney, where the deluge reappears, gradually increasing in intensity and freakishness, culminating in a downpour of frogs.

Scientific attempts to explain the strange weather conditions are unimportant in this film and are made just twice, and then only over the radio. The announcer quotes weather experts explaining that "the situation has been caused by an unusual widespread low pressure trough moving up from the southern polar ice." Although scientific explanations are characteristic of the science fiction genre, the manner in which they are employed in *The Last Wave* does not prompt the viewer to perceive the film as a mystery to be explained in scientific terms. Instead of building the atmosphere around efforts to resolve mystery, this film, like *Picnic at Hanging Rock,* reveals the futility of rational explanation when confronted with the mysteries of nature.

Taking this and other elements associated with the creation of horror (for instance, scenes that take place in the city's underground Aboriginal caves, black figures standing in the rain outside of the protagonist's house) into account, Weir's film shares some similarities with horror films in which questions referring to scientific (or, rather, pseudoscientific) explanations of supernatural events are irrelevant, and, furthermore, in which scientists and their quasi-inventions are the primary target of this genre's antiscientism. Nevertheless, if analyzed in terms of its plot, pattern, and generic icons, *The Last Wave* would be more of an anthropological thriller, mystery, or atmospheric film than a typical horror film.

Polish critic Piotr Zawojski discusses *The Last Wave* in terms of its similarity to the literary world of magic realism, namely novels by Miguel Angel Asturias, Alejo Carpenter, Gabriel García Márquez, and others. The world of *The Last Wave,* believes Zawojski, cannot be characterized as belonging to either the realistic or the fantastic

realm but as an amalgamation of both, which possesses a coherent inner structure and autonomy.[1] Similarly, for the Australian Adrian Martin, Weir's film deals exclusively with the marvelous by employing Aboriginal dreamtime mythology. Any attempt to explain strange phenomena is peripheral and redundant in this realm.[2]

From the very first scene Weir tries to blur the line between the real and the dreamlike, between the Western World of logic and Aboriginal tribal lore. The film's central figure, David Burton (Richard Chamberlain), a young, successful, middle-class lawyer, is asked by a colleague to defend a group of inner-city Aborigines accused of killing their clan member, Billy Corman (Athol Compton), for stealing the tribal sacred stones. Corman is murdered by an old Aboriginal man, whom the viewer later identifies as Charlie (played by Nandjiwarra Amagula, in real life the spiritual leader of the Aboriginal Groote Eylandt community), who points a "death bone" at him. This initial idea enables Weir to contrast two different worlds, the Aborigines' with their dreamtime and the white Australians' with their rationalized dreams. As is the case in his earlier films, Weir constructs *The Last Wave* around a number of sharp oppositions:

> Whites versus Aborigines
> Real time versus dreamtime
> "Civilized" law versus tribal law
> The rational versus the irrational
> Knowledge versus Magic

Weir depicts the profound division between the white and Aboriginal cultures by constantly juxtaposing them: the official, functionary world of whites is again and again contrasted with the subterranean world of the Aborigines, symbolically located beneath the city sewers. The Aborigines are also a reminder of the complex, unsolved racial problems in contemporary Australia.

In speaking of his intentions during the making of the film, Weir comments: "I wanted in the film to show the contrast between the European without the dreaming and the tribal person with the dreaming" (Mathews, 9/). Weir's film emphasizes an exceptional case of cultural clash, namely a white lawyer's confrontation with the representatives of the Aboriginal inhabitants of Australia. David's wife, Annie (Olivia Hamnett), even explains that she is fourth-generation Australian and has never met an Aborigine before. Consequently, she

A middle-class Australian lawyer (Richard Chamberlain) explores Aboriginal art beneath the streets of Sydney in *The Last Wave* (1977).

is scared of the Aborigines seeking her husband's legal aid, especially of the enigmatic Charlie, who appears in front of her house.

The choice of the profession of lawyer for the protagonist, with its connotations of logic and rational thinking, is not accidental. The contrast between the "civilized" law and the Aboriginal law enables Weir to show the immense cultural gap between the two cultures. In the courtroom scene, in particular, the camera captures the incompatibility of both cultures/laws by juxtaposing close-ups of barristers' white wigs with the black faces of the Aborigines. The scene in which oaths are taken on the Bible, an act that obviously holds no value for the natives, also shows the deep gulf between the rational and the tribal/supernatural.

David, who eventually develops some appreciation for the Aboriginal world of dream but is never able to enter it, slowly becomes convinced that he is a *mulkrul*. According to Aboriginal beliefs, the *mulkrul* is a descendant of the ancient South American race that

inhabited Australia in prehistoric times (David himself was born in South America). In a too-explicit scene, when asked by the Aboriginal elder, Charlie, about his origins, David confirms his role as a *mulkrul,* as a mediator between races who is able to foresee the apocalypse, a person who has "incredible premonitory dreams," an individual belonging to "a race of spirits from the rising sun," as the anthropologist in the film (Vivean Gray) explains to David. From the anthropologist's lengthy comments the viewer also learns that, according to Aboriginal convictions, life is divided into cycles, and "each cycle ends in a kind of apocalypse, usually natural disaster." The reappearance of *mulkruls,* supposedly, signals the end of a cycle and the end of the world.

Since childhood, David Burton has been haunted by nightmares and hallucinations about people who come and steal one's body during sleep. As his stepfather, a clergyman, reminds him, David was also able to predict the death of his mother. In his nightmarish dreams he sees an Aborigine showing him a mysteriously painted stone and a

Richard Chamberlain (David Burton) with David Gulpilil (Chris Lee) in *The Last Wave* (1977).

medicine man sometimes disguised as an owl. David is also troubled by a premonition of a giant apocalyptic flood. When he recognizes one of the Aborigines, Chris, as a figure from his dreams, his anxiety begins to grow. The distressed protagonist sends his family to the country and, with the help of Chris, discovers Aboriginal paintings in the sewers below Sydney that depict an apocalyptic tidal wave. He also uncovers a death mask bearing a strong resemblance to himself. It reinforces his sense of conviction that he is, in fact, a man of two worlds, a *mulkrul*. Through a sewer pipe he gets to the empty Bondi beach and waits there for the inevitable disaster. Finally, he has a vision (or is it real?) of a giant wave, as portended in the film's title.

David's dreams foreshadow later events ("What you dreamed, happened," explains his father) and put him in contact with the Aboriginal dreamtime. *The Last Wave* is consistent in building up tension, as well as in depicting the alienation and emotional entrapment of the protagonist. Weir consciously gives up many traditional cinematic techniques so characteristic of horror and science fiction films. For example, he avoids scenes that might threaten the audience, making no use of sharp turns, shocking imagery, sound effects, and so forth to energize the action. Rather, he employs a slow, gradual, Hitchcockian sense of pacing. This is evident in his portrayal of the lawyer: David's loss of control over his immediate surroundings is gradual. Like most Weir protagonists, the lawyer finds himself in a situation beyond his comprehension and control. Caught between two worlds, the worlds of dream and reality, he is incapable of distinguishing between them. The last sequence, in spite of its explicitness, merely multiplies unanswered questions concerning this dream/reality bond.

On a macro (social) level, *The Last Wave* is a film about a clash of cultures, about the relationship between dream and reality; on a micro (personal) level, it is a psychological journey into the self, ending in a state approaching schizophrenia. David grows increasingly obsessed with his role as mediator between two cultures. It is a task beyond his capabilities. His emotional distress and his subsequent disintegration are natural consequences of the situation. From this perspective, the film in its entirety can be taken as the protagonist's schizophrenic vision: the viewer follows David as he gradually loses all sense of time, becomes isolated from the external world, and eventually falls into madness.

The motif of water, introduced in the first sequence, permeates the film and contributes immensely to its mood. Russell Boyd's camera

catches Aboriginal figures emerging from the torrential rains, shots of the city through David's windshield—Sydney's streets filled with water, David's nightmarish watery hallucination, freaks of nature. Falling water is used to integrate various subplots into a coherent whole: the sprinkler whispers on David's lawn while he discusses his dreams with his stepfather; water drips as Billy Corman's body is examined in the mortuary. Weir even makes fun of his method of building the film's atmosphere and, at the same time, of the audience's expectations by showing a family dinner disrupted by water flowing down the staircase, presumably the result of a child's overflowing bath.

The visual motif of water is most fully developed in the lawyer's apocalyptic visions. Through his car window he sees the streets of Sydney underwater: dead bodies and tomatoes flow by in a dreamy, surrealistic scene. Employing slow motion and using blocks of silence interrupted only by the whir of windshield wipers, Weir achieves a remarkably hallucinatory and nightmarish effect.

Perhaps coincidentally, water imagery also plays a significant role in *The Plumber* (his profession concerns water), *Gallipoli* (soldiers swim underwater), *The Year of Living Dangerously* (a pool scene), and *The Mosquito Coast* (rivers, coastlines, seas). In *The Last Wave,* however, the motif of water is used as the major element, the overriding motif connecting plot elements and establishing atmosphere. In comparison with the soft, sunny, lyrical colors of *Picnic at Hanging Rock,* *The Last Wave* is cold, dark, bathed in rain; the colors (mostly blacks, browns, and greens) heighten the sense of menace and isolation felt by the protagonist.

In fact, *The Last Wave* suffers from excessive explicitness. Despite its visual beauty, it is too verbal and too literal. Its cinematic sophistication does not balance its narrative shallowness. Weir too often employs verbal comments to explain the plot; he cannot refrain from naming things. This policy rigidifies the film, closing both the narrative line and the ideas contained within it. *The Last Wave* lacks tension in some crucial scenes in which Weir relies heavily on the verbal commentary of the protagonists rather than building tension and atmosphere by using strong visual images, as is characteristic in his other works. In comparison with the enigmatic lines from *Picnic at Hanging Rock,* some dialogue passages in *The Last Wave* weaken the atmosphere of mystery. The protagonists talk about dreams, laws, and mysteries. The weakness of the screenplay (written by Weir with Tony Morphett and Petru Popescu) prevents Weir from reaching his

full potential. On the one hand, the film is superficial in its exploration of the plight of Aborigines in urban society and, hence, fails to
function as an accurate reflection of social pressures. On the other
hand, it is too literal to maintain the tension that is part and parcel of
the mystery film. Weir usually chooses to make the endings of his
films enigmatic,[3] but the final sequence here is heavy-handed, too
obviously symbolic, as David awaits the wave on the beach. The ending breaks the rules established at the beginning of the film and
makes visible what should be hidden within it.

Weir's film as a whole may be taken as a visualization of the protagonist's nightmarish dream. In *The Last Wave,* it is only possible to comprehend mystery within the realm of dreams. This is also strongly
emphasized in *Picnic at Hanging Rock:* the girls go to sleep on the
rock, awaken, continue their exploration, and never return; Michael
sleeps on the rock and then is able to find Irma; Albert's sister,
unknown to him, appears in his dreams. *The Last Wave* also looks like
the protagonist's dream: while preparing for a complex legal procedure, he has a dream about his alleged affinity with the incomprehensible—that is, in terms of traditional rational thought, Aboriginal
culture. *The Last Wave* thus serves as a clear example of what might
be perceived as a realization in cinematic form of the theories of Carl
Gustav Jung.[4]

   For Jung, dreams emerge not only from the dreamer's buried psy-
chic life but from archetypal elements common to all cultures. In his
dream analysis, Jung asserts that there is material in dreams that could
never originate in personal experience but that must be derived from
archaic levels of the mind, the source of which can be found in
humanity's primitive ancestry and in the experience of the race. Furthermore, he believes that within each person there is a "collective
unconscious" that makes itself known through "primordial images."
The forms in which these "primordial images" manifest themselves
in conscious life Jung denominates as archetypal images.

   The concept of dreams as unifying all cultures and races and the
concept of archetypes common to all human beings pervades Weir's
film. In interviews Weir often stresses the importance of Jung's writings together with works by authors who span several disciplines:
Thor Heyerdahl and Emmanuel Velikovsky (Mathews, 113; McFarlane and Ryan, 325). Weir comments that Jung's archetypal images
"came together for [him] around the time [he] was finishing the
script of *The Last Wave,* and a lot of that material, [he] found, could

be looked at from a Jungian perspective."[5] A faithful reader of Jung, Weir makes his protagonist a dreamer, able not only to foresee future events but also, thanks to dreams, to experience spiritual nearness to a different culture.

In addition to archetypal images and dreams, the similarity between dream and film has influenced many artists, including Weir. Since the beginning of cinema, both filmmakers and audiences have addressed this parallel. The dreamlike quality of cinematic depiction typically results in films being perceived by critics as visualizations of dreams. Weir's film, however, does not appear to be either his or the audience's dreams but is rather structured like a dream. The director does not translate the language of dreams into cinematic images; his interest lies in creating an oneiric mood. Both the narrative and the visual levels of *The Last Wave* diminish the distinction between real and dreamlike worlds. The viewers' identification with this dreamlike atmosphere and consequent associations with their own dreams intensifies the impact of the film.

Weir's preoccupation with dream, however, makes him neglectful of social commentary on the situation of the native inhabitants of Australia. *The Last Wave,* written and acted in part by Aborigines,[6] merely touches on the "Aboriginal problem." For instance, compared with Phillip Noyce's *Backroads* (1977), Fred Schepisi's *The Chant of Jimmie Blacksmith* (1978), or Ned Lander's *Wrong Side of the Road* (1981), which present Aborigines as victims of the system, Weir romanticizes Aborigines and ignores social issues. *The Last Wave,* however, cannot be described as failing to pay attention to the predicament of Australia's Aboriginal people or as using them as exotic figures in the manner of, for instance, Tim Burstall in *Eliza Frazer* (1976) or later Igor Auzin in *We of the Never Never* (1982).

Weir is more an anthropologist than a political scientist. For him, the clash of two different cultures is simply an opportunity to explore their incompatibility and their inability to understand each other. As a rule, Weir romanticizes "primitive" people; such a treatment in *The Last Wave* hinders the film from speaking more seriously about the plight of Aborigines in contemporary Australia. In spite of the native actors and their important contribution, the film falls into a romantic conclusion about the superiority of Aboriginal "primitive" culture over white rationalized culture, the latter of which is devoid of dreams. (Ironically, the protagonist of this film is accused by his friends from Legal Aid of having fallen prey to "idiotic romantic

crap" and "middle-class paternalism" toward the Aborigines; more-over, David is persuaded that "there are no tribal people in the city" and, consequently, that the killing of Billy Corman has no tribal significance and cannot be given to tribal authorities.)

The Last Wave draws on the same conventional images of Aboriginal people that can be found in many of the New Wave Australian films. The Aborigines in contemporary Australian cinema are primarily presented as exotic figures of mysterious power lost in a white man's world, people with a special understanding of secrets of nature, a tribal culture that relies heavily on its dreamtime mythology. The presence of Aboriginal people in Australian films, mostly as the protagonist's sidekick, guiding him through the impenetrable interior landscape, is used to enhance the films' sense of "Australianess."

Contrary to the viewer's expectations, however, Weir's film belongs to a comparatively small group of Australian feature films dealing with the country's native inhabitants. In discussing Australian films made before 1977 (before *The Last Wave*), Andrew Pike explains the peculiar situation in which "minorities of most types, whether racial, social or political, have rarely received more than peripheral attention from the commercial mainstream of Australian cinema, which has always been the domain of the white urban middle class."[7]

Since the inception of the local film industry, the Aborigines have been presented in many films, but until the appearance of Charles Chauvel's *Jedda* (1955), they were treated as marginal, exotic figures populating equally exotic outback landscapes. The Aborigines appeared frequently in the bushranging genre, mostly as faithful helper-friends to the heroic/romantic figure of the bushranger. In many respects, the treatment of Aboriginal people in Australian films is analogous to the portrayal of American Indians and African Americans in Hollywood films. As in American films, Aborigines were often played by white actors made up with black faces.[8] However, there is one feature that differentiates them from Native Americans and African Americans: there always was and still is sympathy (perhaps a sense of guilt?) toward Aborigines as outsiders. They function as colorful, yet passive figures unable to threaten white Australians, their role largely limited to two major characteristics. First, they were cast as voiceless savages, and their appearances, as Catriona Moore and Stephen Muecke state, "were indistinguishable from those of blacks in Tarzan-type movies."[9] Second, the Aborigines were and still are nearly synonymous with the Australian landscape, or rather, con-

stitute a "natural" component of that landscape. They are frequently nonpersons: dehumanized, mythlike figures stereotypically portrayed against the background of a sunset or at rest beneath a gum tree. In discussing this issue, Graeme Turner points out,

> Aborigines have been, and continue to be seen as metonyms for an Australian landscape; like kangaroos and Ayers Rock, they are among the natural attributes of the continent. This is dehumanizing, and has served to legitimate white settlers' treatment of the Aborigines as pests well into the twentieth century. It is also a way of displacing the social and political problems. To see the Aboriginal as a dying species rather than a subordinated culture is to explain their condition as a result of the inevitable operation of natural forces rather than as the product of a specific history.[10]

Turner's point here is of great importance. An inability to come to terms with the "Aboriginal issue" creates a peculiar situation in which, no matter how noble and "progressive" intentions are, film-makers tend to employ the Aborigine figure only as an emblem of "natural," almost biological forces and as an archetype deprived of individuality. Contrary to most films' white protagonists, Aborigines symbolize the land and its prehistory. A sense of guilt toward Aborigines is behind many attempts at rewriting Australian history from a "more objective" perspective. Frequently, however, the result is a disappointing image of a powerful Aboriginal culture, richer in many aspects than the Western culture, the image being a product of romantic representation and guilt-ridden sentimentality rather than a reflection of history and present-day reality. The majority of the attempts made by filmmakers at depicting the Aboriginal culture can still be described as an act of "intellectual tourism," a term coined by Turner to describe the attempts by white academics to go beyond their ideological framework while deconstructing white Australia's construction of Aboriginal culture (Turner, 135).

A similar problem arises in Australian fiction dealing with the "Aboriginal issue." The Aborigines were first introduced as a problem for the white settlers.[11] From the colonizers' point of view, they were usually presented as either threatening Stone Age nomads or noble savages lost in a white world. The evolution of the portrayal of Aborigines can be described as a shift from presenting them as aggressors and a threat to capitalist progress to presenting them as victims of social injustice imposed by white colonization. An analogous change is also noticeable in contemporary Australian cinema to

the point where Aborigines are presented as either tragic, humiliated figures taking desperate revenge for injustice done to them (*The Chant of Jimmie Blacksmith*) or dignified figures shown in a sentimental-romantic fashion (*The Last Wave*).

In discussing the way in which Aboriginal people are presented on the screen, Moore and Muecke distinguish three "discursive formations," linked with Australian cultural policy, that characterize Australian films containing images of Aborigines (Moore and Muecke, 36). The "paternalistic assimilationist" formation characterizes films made in the 1950s and 1960s. It was followed by a "liberal multiculturalist" formation, present up to now, that portrays the Aboriginal culture as one of many national cultures contributing to the "mosaic" of Australian culture. The third formation, parallel to the "multiculturalist" one, deals with independent films made by Aboriginal filmmakers from their own perspective. If we accept the above-mentioned periodization, *The Last Wave,* with its idealist concept of dreaming, defies categorization. Moore and Muecke, however, see this and other "Aboriginal films" made in the 1970s as a result of "liberalizing the frontier" (Moore and Muecke, 42–43).

The Last Wave, like its predecessor, *Picnic at Hanging Rock,* is a film with a rare sense of mystery. On the surface, both films contain a loose narrative line, but in fact both have a coherent inner logic.

The Last Wave and *Picnic at Hanging Rock* deal with dream and the possibility of crossing the border between the rational and the spiritual; their protagonists act within the borderland of these two worlds and unsuccessfully try to mediate between them. The two films, working with similar material, achieve different results. Mysterious from the beginning to the end, *Picnic at Hanging Rock* relies on its strong impressionistic visual images and haunting music and is nearly a pure "atmospheric film." It offers no explanation for its mystery. *The Last Wave* appears to point to Weir's disbelief in the audience's ability to comprehend: it is overly explicit and less dreamlike; it offers an explanation. Nonetheless, the importance of *The Last Wave* lies in its creation of a dreamlike atmosphere purely via cinematic techniques. The first part of the film in particular, which owes a great deal to special effects (by Monty Fieguth and Robert Hilditch) and Boyd's photography, serves as a good example of Weir's ability to create an unsettling mood. Unfortunately, the film loses its impetus and the weakness of the screenplay surfaces. *The Last Wave's* visual greatness is not matched by its explicit narrative.

CHAPTER 5

The Quest for Self-Identity: *Gallipoli*

If there had not been a Gallipoli, Australians would have invented it.
—Livio and Pat Dobrez,
"Old Myths and New Delusions: Peter Weir's Australia"

Gallipoli (1981) was "my graduation film," stated Peter Weir, treating this work as the end product of the period when he was particularly interested in myths and dreams.[1] *Gallipoli,* one of the masterpieces of Australian cinema, is also Weir's most Australian film. It is evidence of his search for the roots of national identity in the World War I battle of Gallipoli—a battle of marginal significance to the outcome of the war overall but of great significance to Australians' perception of themselves.

This "graduation" also suggests a turn toward professionalism and filmic maturity. And it signals a move away from low-budget films made in his own country toward high-budget films made in the United States that reflect a style common to American film production. Furthermore, Weir's "graduation" and the making of *Gallipoli* indicate a turn toward simplicity and clarity, toward concentration on a specific genre in each film, a shift from the mysterious oneiric landscape of *Picnic at Hanging Rock* and *The Last Wave*. With George Miller's *Mad Max* (1979), *Gallipoli* was also one of the first Australian films to receive mainstream American distribution (by Paramount).

In his 1986 interview with *Film Comment,* Weir once again emphasized the importance of *Gallipoli* in his artistic development.

For him, it was a breakthrough film that came after one year of studying European and American cinema. *Gallipoli* is also his "least personal film" and his favorite one. "It was the first time," he claims, "I think I had real confidence in what I was doing, some understanding of craft, while still being an apprentice" (McGilligan, 30).

As opposed to Weir's earlier films, *Gallipoli* is based on authentic historical events, the participation of Anzac (Australian and New Zealand) troops in the 1915 Dardanelles campaign. Australian and New Zealand troops landed on the Aegean side of the Gallipoli peninsula near the end of April 1915 and fought there through December 1915, when the troops were evacuated. The film's climax is the suicidal, senseless attack on well-fortified Turkish trenches undertaken by the eighth and tenth Light Horse Regiments of Anzacs. "The wireless tells and the cable tells, how our boys behaved by the Dardanelles," Henry Lawson begins his famous "Song of the Dardanelles."[2] Nevertheless, the film is not simply an attempt to reconstruct those events but deals with Weir's favorite theme—that of individuals facing strange events in a hostile environment. This metaphysical cast of theme gives way to a psychosociological approach that finds reflection in Weir's choice of thematic opposition. The cosmic oppositions of Weir's earlier films—dream versus reality (*The Last Wave*), nature versus culture (*Picnic at Hanging Rock*)—are replaced by a more concrete dichotomy in *Gallipoli*: Australia versus Great Britain.

The purpose of the film is to define the notion of "the Australian nation" by reconsidering stereotype and myth: the notion of the good Australian versus the bad foreigner, of Australia as innocent, of Australianess versus Britishness. Employing visual stereotypes, Weir does not want to deconstruct but rather to reinforce the mythic elements constituting the Australian national identity. Such a cinematic purpose was strongly advocated by Phillip Adams, one of the leading advocates for the creation of national cinema: "We got into this industry for one reason: to give ourselves a national voice, to give ourselves a sense of national purpose and a national identity, and to throw it that way would be a disaster and a fiasco."[3]

Of course, Weir's film is not the first artifact to play on the modern Australian self-image. *Gallipoli* is deeply rooted in the local mythology of Australia as well as in the national traditions of literature and painting. And as such, Weir's film may be seen both to derive from and continue the discussions on national identity as well as nationalist feeling, which emerged distinctively for the first time by the end

of the nineteenth century. The changing attitude toward the Australian landscape, the romanticization of the bush and the bushman,
and the emergence of local artists, painters, poets, and writers interested in defining their new environment contributed to the nation-
making process. Finally, the Boer War, which was under British com-
mand but included Australian participation, was a kind of "emotional
substitute for a real war of independence."[4] The war correspondent
and poet A. A. G. "Smiler" Hales put it bluntly:

> A nation is never a nation
> Worthy of pride or place
> Till the mothers have sent their first born
> To look death in the field in the face. (Eddy and Schreuder, 153)

The Gallipoli battle has an important place in Australian history and
mythology. Bill Gammage, historian and adviser on the film, notes
that before Gallipoli, in November 1914, the Australian cruiser *Sydney* had driven aground the German light cruiser *Emden*. This victory was celebrated as conferring adulthood on the Australian navy.
To build a nation, however, a more spectacular event was needed.
"The time was awaiting the event," concludes Gammage.[5]

Despite its title, *Gallipoli* is not a "war film" or an "antiwar film"
but a "celebration of the national ideology," as Jane Freebury
observes in her symptomatically subtitled article "Screening Australia—*Gallipoli:* A Study of Nationalism on Film."[6] The film emphasizes the parallels between personal and national history. The protagonists, Archy Hamilton (Mark Lee) and Frank Dunne (Mel Gibson),
resemble Australia itself—young, inexperienced, enthusiastic. In the
first part of *Gallipoli,* Archy's trainer, Uncle Jack (Bill Kerr), reads to
his family passages from Kipling's *Jungle Book,* in which Mowgli
becomes a man. Later, for Archy and Frank, the Gallipoli battle marks
their passage into manhood, and for Australia, the baptism of fire and,
consequently, the birth of a nation. Albinoni's funereal Adagio for
Strings and Organ serves to emphasize this painful moment.

Weir's film contrasts the essence of Australianess (mateship, the
outback, isolation, innocence) with the corruption, depravity, and
crowdedness of the rest of the world. Australia's isolation from the
world's issues and hence its innocence is strongly stressed, particularly
in the first part of the film, which takes place in Western Australia's
outback. The key scene of Archy and Frank's meeting with an old
man with a camel in the desert emphasizes this distinctly. The old

man, Stumpy (Harold Baigent), does not know about the war and has never been to Perth. When Archy explains why Australians are involved in the war, the old man cannot understand. Weir's (and scriptwriter David Williamson's) sense of humor puts it this way: "Still, can't see what it's got to do with us," says Stumpy. "If we don't stop them they could end up here," responds Archy. "And they are welcome to it," Stumpy concludes, looking around at the vast desolate countryside. Weir conveys Australia's sense of isolation by emphasizing the emptiness and immensity of the landscape.

In combining themes of isolation and images of landscape, Weir accentuates an aspect central to the Australian mythology of self-identity. As a rule, the Australian landscape is one of the most important elements of the New Wave period films. *Picnic at Hanging Rock, Sunday Too Far Away, The Mango Tree* (1977), *The Chant of Jimmie Blacksmith, The Irishman* (1978), *My Brilliant Career* (1979), and many others employ the landscape to generate the essence of Australia. The Australian landscape in these films is the source of meaning—a distinctive characteristic that has its own discursive function. It typifies the "real Australia" and establishes the difference between Australian and European culture.

There was always a visible duality in Australian artists' representation of their landscape. One group of artists, particularly those with European backgrounds, perceived the land as hostile and dangerous, constituted of an alien nature. Another group of artists tried to capture the uniqueness of the land and to depict its physical environment, promoting and even idealizing the land. Exploring their physical environment, they attempted to overcome the "colonial inferiority complex." The change from a colonial to a national art was linked primarily with a different perception of the landscape: from alien and hostile to human and mythic, with marked preference for the local Australian over the English imperial.

As mentioned in chapter 3, it was the Heidelberg School of impressionist painting, which flourished between 1885 and 1890, that established popular images of the rural Australian landscape, rejecting the colonial painters' vision of a strange new continent. As early as 1875, however, William Ford had painted his *Picnic at Hanging Rock near Macedon,* which depicts Victorian families resting in an Eden-like Australian bush. Representatives of the Heidelberg School (Tom Roberts, Frederick McCubbin, Charles Conder, and others) not only depicted effects of light and color but introduced and interpreted the Australian sunlit landscape. McCubbin's *The Lost Child*

(1886), also mentioned in chapter 3, can be seen as a metaphor for Europeans in Australia, showing a child dressed in blue-green colors and visually camouflaged among gum trees. This motif often appeared in Australian paintings and prints, for instance, in the popular prints of Samuel Thomas Gill (*The Australian Sketchbook,* 1865). Later painters, most notably Sydney Nolan, Russell Drysdale, and Arthur Boyd, stressed the uniqueness of the landscape and its metaphysical and mythic content. The landscape thus became mythologized and perceived as distinctively Australian.

Australian writers were also concerned with explaining and promoting their environment. Like the painters, they created a charmed picture of the rural lifestyle while describing Australia's non-European landscape. In particular, the bush and the bushman stood for the "real Australia." The change from a colonial to a national literature was connected with a specific shift of emphasis: from nostalgia for Europe and a related representation of the outback simply as an exotic background for novels of European experience (in the writings of Ada Cambridge or Rosa Campbell Praed, for instance), to national awareness, to the situation in which the bush is seen as distinctively Australian and hence idealized, as in the works of Henry Lawson, Andrew Barton "Banjo" Paterson, Miles Franklin, Joseph Furphy, and Bernard O'Dowd.

Given this history of a consciously articulated attempt to emphasize the specificity of Australian geography and experience in cultural expression, it is perhaps inevitable that these expressions should take on a mythic dimension to become, like the Australian landscape itself, larger than life. "Australia is a small country with long journeys," states George Seddon.[7] Russell Boyd's photography in *Gallipoli* stresses the emptiness of the landscape. The monochromatic sandy colors of three deserts—Australian, Egyptian, and Turkish (Gallipoli)—and the khaki color of the soldiers' uniforms, contrasted with a blue sky, dominate the film. The oneiric images of young men crossing the Australian desert, night scenes under the pyramids, the landing at Gallipoli, the underwater scene there, and many others enhance the atmosphere of Weir's film. They re-create more myth than historical reality.

Similar to the protagonists of *Picnic at Hanging Rock* and *The Last Wave,* those in *Gallipoli* move toward something unknown, an undefined force. When they reach the finale, one of them, the innocent virginal Archy, loses his life. Although *Gallipoli* is not a "mystery film," its mythic content, enhanced by carefully used cinematic

devices, produces a dreamlike effect. The historical inaccuracies of the film are entirely subordinated to newly arisen myth.

The landscape in the first part of *Gallipoli,* many times reproduced in earlier Australian films, sets the visual tone. In the desert scene, crucial to the film's presentation of Australia's isolation in 1915, Weir employs the immensity of the landscape and juxtaposes it with the boys' youthfulness, enthusiasm, and desire to see the world. If in *Picnic at Hanging Rock* and *The Last Wave* the director plays on the theme of nature versus culture, in *Gallipoli* he stresses the unity of man and the landscape that is only seemingly hostile to man. Like American film director John Ford, who created in his films an archetypal landscape of the American West, Weir sees the landscape as the source of meaning. Although at first human figures seem alienated from the landscape, ultimately they are neither powerless nor insignificant. On the contrary, human beings, in taming the landscape, are precisely what established a mythology of both the American West and the Australian outback.

Weir chooses the outback as a starting point for his film, as is the case with most successful Australian films of the 1970s. Although Australia is one of the most urbanized countries in the world (most Australians still live only in a few large coastal cities), one of Weir's protagonists (Archy) comes from the countryside (the bush), which symbolizes the "true Australia," based on a male-dominated society. The Australian rural worker (the bushman) embodies the ideal Australian. Weir contrasts rural virtues with the decadence and moral corruption of the city. Frank, the working-class Irish boy from the city (larrikin/ocker), has become corrupted by the city. He can be saved only by his relationship with a noble bushman. This contrast between urban and rural life, which the director later employed in *Witness* (1985), is present in the Australian cinema from its beginnings. In his *Legends on the Screen,* John Tulloch shows that the thematic concern of Australian cinema in the 1920s was to establish the contrast between the city and the bush. He goes on to suggest that this opposition replaced the class antagonism of Australian society.[8] Interestingly, this same opposition is the source of the international success of such films as Paul Hogan's *Crocodile Dundee* (1986), which play on the distinction between the rural Australian and urban American.

In *The Australian Legend,* Russel Ward tries to explain the role of the Australian landscape and the role of the bush in film and literature in terms of the "frontier theory" elaborated by the American

historian F. J. Turner.[9] *The Australian Legend* draws on literature, folk songs, and other historical documents to trace and explain the development of the Australian self-image. In Ward's view, the real Australian is the inheritor of the legacy of the last century's bushmen, whose prestige—if not their number—was always greater than that of city dwellers. An answer to the problem of why such prestige should have been afforded the bushman in Australian culture is partly suggested by Turner's frontier theory. Before Turner, historians tended to explain the American past with reference to European influences. His achievement was to show how "frontier influences" were no less important to an understanding of the local history. According to Ward, the Australian outback performed the same function as the American frontier: it helped to develop national cohesion. For America, the frontier is the West and its pioneers; for Australia, it is the landscape of the interior and the bushman, a folk hero who epitomizes the national character, the hero whose lifestyle and values differ from those of other nations. Like American pioneers, bushmen entered and conquered an alien landscape. They tamed a hostile environment, made it human, and thus performed a central civilizing, nation-building function. For Ward, the myth of the Australian frontier and frontiersman promoted the growth of nationalism and shaped the present-day stereotypes of so-called typical Australian behavior. According to Ward, the romanticization of the bush was promoted by nationalists who wanted to establish the difference between British and Australian culture.

In contemporary Australian cinema there is a conscious preoccupation with producing images that focus on the "Australian experience" and that celebrate "Australianess." In his *Australian Cinema, 1970–1985,* Brian McFarlane discusses images commonly projected by Australian films of the 1970s and the 1980s: a country populated by white men, mateship, antiauthoritarianism, the landscape ("a wide brown land"), individuals facing difficulties without complaining about them or giving up ("battlers"), and the competitive spirit.[10] As with most Australian films dealing with the past, Weir employs all of these important elements of national identity and promotes them.

In *Gallipoli,* Weir develops the discourse on mateship by showing that the young men's rivalry and different attitudes toward war originate in their different family backgrounds. "It's not our bloody war," says Frank. "It's an English war—it's got nothing to do with us." His father also tells him not to fight for the English, who murdered his grandfather "five miles from Dublin." This attitude toward the war

recalls a well-known stanza of Henry Lawson's "The Ballad of the Cornstalk," in which he writes about the Boer War:

> I'm going to the war, and I don't know what it's for,
> But the other chaps are going with the Bush Contingent men,
> And if I should stay behind, there'll be trouble in the wind
> For my girl will throw me over when they come back agen.[11]

Unlike Frank, Archy has grown up in a family with strong pro-British feelings. His joining the Light Horse is, apart from an opportunity to change his life, an answer to the call: "The Empire needs you!"

The mateship motif, frequently present in Australian cinema and dramatized by Weir in the relationship between Archy and Frank, is the leading motif of *Gallipoli*.[12] Mateship has a mythological character in Australia; it defines the Australian male self-image. Always at the center of this myth is the bushman. In *The Australian Legend,* Ward compares the character of the Australian soldier and the character of the bushman: "Comradeship and loyalty, resourcefulness and adaptability are as necessary to the one life as to the other. And just as the bushman liked, on principle, to emphasise his 'independence' from his masters, while being sometimes on good terms with the individual squatter, so the digger [the ordinary Australian man] liked to be thought that he cared nothing for officers as a class" (Ward, 231).

Paterson and Lawson, for instance, saw the bushman as the embodiment of all Australian virtues. They mythologize him and mateship in innumerable poems and stories. In his famous "Shearers," Lawson writes,

> And though he may be brown or black,
>   Or wrong man there, or right man,
> The mate that's steadfast to his mates
>   They call that man a "white man!"
> They tramp in mateship side by side—
>   The Protestant and Roman—
> They call no biped lord or sir,
>   And touch their hat to no man![13]

And thus, not surprisingly, the myth of Gallipoli and the myth of Australia are about white men. The landscape of *Gallipoli* is reserved for men—there seems to be no place for women in the Big Aus-

tralian Myth. Their place is taken by mates. Characteristically, as Brian McFarlane points out in *Australian Cinema,* "If the mateship is no longer an important motif in Australian literature, several films of the past decade have helped to reinforce the myth" (McFarlane 1987, 54). Some of the best-known Australian films incorporate this motif into their narratives: *Sunday Too Far Away, Breaker Morant* (1980), and *The Lighthorsemen* (1987).

Archy and Frank's friendship, beginning with their first athletic rivalry, the Freemantle race, is continued throughout the film. Its dramatization enables Weir to develop a personal story instead of a historical epic. He personalizes history and thus indicates concern with its human aspect.

Another important element of the Australian national identity, antiauthoritarianism, is presented in this film as an anti-British feeling. Weir claims that "the larger issue is not the anti-British viewpoint, but the pro-Australian viewpoint" (Fonda Bonardi, 42), though these two elements are inseparably linked in the film. British

Mark Lee (left, as Archy Hamilton) and Mel Gibson (Frank Dunne) in *Gallipoli* (1981).

officers are caricaturized as monocled and mustachioed cynics, their treatment of Anzac troops as unfair. The British officer comments on Australians who ape him riding on donkeys: "You Australians are crude, undisciplined, and the most ill-mannered soldiers I've ever encountered." The Anzacs' sacrifice is contrasted with the selfishness of the British, who are "just sitting on the beach drinking cups of tea." Ultimately, the British are blamed for the massacre of Australians. Likewise, Bruce Beresford in his finest Australian film, *Breaker Morant,* while showing Australian participation in the Boer War, employs many anti-British stereotypes to elicit a sympathetic and positive attitude from the viewer toward Australians. Historical complexity is not essential here; through the use of melodramatic conventions, *Breaker Morant* works as a powerful political statement, creating an image of "the scapegoats of the Empire."

Many of these same negative stereotypes of Englishmen can be traced to early bush balladists' verses. For instance, Lawson, in "A New John Bull," describes an English gentleman who "shakes hands like a ladies' man," "hates to soil his hands," "removes the grime of gunpowder and polishes his nails." Lawson concludes ironically,

> Although he never showed a sign
> of aught save sympathy
> He was the only gentleman
> That shamed the lout in me. (Lawson 1964, 43)

In his *Social Patterns in Australian Literature,* Tom Inglis Moore convincingly elucidates the complex social circumstances underlying English-Australian hostility: "The cultural clash was sharpened by the discord between English and Australian manners and speech. The educated English settler was repelled by the colonial informality, crudity, and coarseness. The native colonial in turn usually scorned refinement as an unmanly affectation of the English gentry and preferred to be 'rough but honest,' illogically equating the two and suspecting the sincerity of anyone refined."[14]

In expanding on the negative image of the Englishman, while simultaneously creating and emphasizing the innocence of Australia (characteristically, the most innocent among Australian soldiers is named Snowy), Weir posits the outside world in its entirety as aggressive (embodied in war), dishonest (embodied by British officers), corrupt (in the Cairo scene), and marked by death (the scene at Gallipoli). To further generate the sense of Australia's innocence, Weir

includes in *Gallipoli* a sequence showing soldiers being recruited to the Light Horse. A wooden Trojan-like horse, symbol of cunning as well as imposture, appears bearing the appeal, "Join the Light Horse!" A similar point of view regarding the innocence of Australia as opposed to the corruption of the outside world is shared by Bill Gammage, whose book *The Broken Years* (1974), based on the diaries and letters of one thousand Australian soldiers during the Gallipoli campaign, emphasizes the ways in which the innocence of the Australian soldiers clashed with the severe laws of an alien war.[15]

Both Weir and Williamson admit that their inspiration while working on the film was C. E. W. Bean's official history, *The Story of Anzac from the Outbreak of War to the End of the First Phase of the Gallipoli Campaign, May 4, 1915,* first published in 1921. According to Bean, at that time an official war correspondent and later a historian, Australian soldiers were the finest in the imperial army thanks to their bushman qualities.[16] This corresponds to Henry Lawson's description of Anzacs in "Song of the Dardanelles" as "the youngest and strongest of England's brood!" (Lawson 1964, 156). C. E. W. Bean argued that the digger at Gallipoli was the product of the bush: "The Australian was half a soldier before the war; indeed throughout the war . . . the Australian soldier differed very little from the Australian who at home rides the station boundaries every week-day" (quoted in White, 132).

Bean also stressed the democratic nature of the Anzac troops. The Australian army was egalitarian. Officers frequently fraternized with their men; they were not separated from soldiers. In the film, Major Barton (Bill Hunter), a fatherly Australian officer, is contrasted with the British officers. Barton cares for his men and is on friendly terms with them. Their final tragedy is also his tragedy. British officers are presented as anachronistic figures, remnants of the declining Empire.

Competitiveness, another mythic aspect of Australia's national identity, is presented starting from the very first sequence of *Gallipoli*. Archy's uncle is training him in a ritual-like fashion to sprint. The same ritual is repeated by Archy at Gallipoli before the final charge toward the Turkish trenches. The long sprint of the protagonist both commences and ends the film. There is, however, another, metaphorical aspect of the race. In Egypt, Archy and Frank race toward the pyramid tombs. Innocence is contrasted with experience and death. In an earlier scene, the camera portrays the Anzacs' camp at night against the pyramids. Australians' tents resemble small pyramid-like tombs. However, the pyramids are not only symbols of death but also

of immortality. Although the Australians' way to the trenches of Gallipoli is marked by joyful moments (the nurses' ball in Egypt, naked Aussies swimming underwater as if removed from the brutal reality of the bombardment above), the viewer is reminded of watching a drama—a powerful drama about virginity lost.

The competitive spirit, as well as Australia's newness, is also strongly emphasized in the famous scene of the Australian rules football match played against the background of the Egyptian pyramids. There is a clash between the young and old cultures, and between naivete and craftiness. Later, at Gallipoli, where everything seems too serious and cruel for the Australians, this spirit is inappropriate; they senselessly die attacking the enemy. A freeze-frame of Archy Hamilton ends the film. This final frame shows one life that was ended too early, but at the same time the freeze-frame symbolizes, preserves, and immortalizes Archy via the cinematic process.

Some critics see similarities between Weir's film and Hugh Hudson's *Chariots of Fire* (1981): both films focus on two runners/mates

Mel Gibson (Frank Dunne) in an unsuccessful attempt to stop the suicidal attack at Gallipoli. From the 1981 film.

whose personalities differ distinctively, and both share similar narrative patterns. Nevertheless, as William J. Palmer states, there is a huge difference between the two films, which is analogous to "the difference between romance and reality . . . *Gallipoli* is *Chariots of Fire* for the real world."[17]

If the battle of Gallipoli marked for Australians the symbolic birth of their nation, Weir's *Gallipoli* plays on the concept of nationhood and the self-image of Australians. Although it does not share the same optimistic, patriotic spirit as does, for instance, Charles Chauvel's *Forty Thousand Horsemen* (1940), *Gallipoli* pays homage to earlier films about Australia's participation in World War I and quotes Chauvel's filmic version of those events. The images of the battle already appeared in Alfred Rolfe's 1915 propaganda feature, *The Hero of the Dardanelles;* repeated many times over in later films, they survived almost untouched. Sylvia Lawson goes so far as to suggest: "There are sixty-six years of history between these two intensely mythic shots [of the soldiers against the Egyptian pyramids at sunset]; there is almost no ideological space between them at all. The first celebrates the Australian soldier; the second that mateship, which, Bean proposed, invigorated their soldiering."[18]

Though Lawson perhaps overstates the case, she is right to point out the conservative character of the local film industry. Weir's film creates the same notions as Chauvel's *Forty Thousand Horsemen;* however, unlike its predecessor, *Gallipoli* reinforces mythic images of what, supposedly, is "Australianess." "In a country with a short history, the few high points become inflated into mythical proportions," says the scriptwriter David Williamson.[19] Weir's film does not intend to discuss conventional issues connected with "war," "patriotism," and "the nation." Instead, it tries to present the essence of the "true Australia"—a mythic, pastoral landscape peopled with mythic characters.

In this attempt, Weir's film corresponds to Sydney Nolan's paintings of Gallipoli. Nolan painted naked Anzacs who bathe on Gallipoli beaches. They are presented not as living but mythic figures of Australian culture. They are archetypes vital to the national legend. Weir's Archy Hamilton and Nolan's diggers function as icons—ahistorical, mythlike figures constituting the Australian psyche.

We are dealing with a country in which language is no longer a distinguishing attribute of national identity. In postcolonial nations, this situation stirs a peculiar need for defining the differences between colonizer and colonized. Local history and local characters are put on a pedestal as "noble, heroic or tragic" (Freebury, 8). All

national cinemas manipulate the audience's emotion with powerful national symbols. Australian cinema is in the process of creating that symbolism by employing stereotypes of the country's current and foundational myths. The main task is to delineate the difference between Australianess and Britishness while still preserving a sense of British heritage. The images from Australian New Wave films do not show Australians as "second-hand Europeans" who "pullulate timidly on the edge on alien shores," as A. D. Hope states in his poem "Australia,"[20] but as descendants of noble bushmen and self-sacrificing diggers at Gallipoli.

Richard White, in his appropriately titled book *Inventing Australia,* demonstrates the changing construction of the national image and the conscious attempt to produce an acceptable image of Australia. In the introduction he makes an explicit point: "A national identity is an invention. There is no point asking whether one version of this essential Australia is truer than another because they are all intellectual constructs, neat, tidy, comprehensible—and necessarily false. They have all been artificially imposed upon a diverse landscape and population, and a variety of untidy social relationships, attitudes and emotions" (White, vii).

The role of the Australian government in "producing Australia" on the screen is crucial. The period film, the reworking of some of the strategies of European art film, was heavily funded by the Australian government in the 1970s. This genre, with its "art cinema" mise-en-scène and traditional narrative, gained cultural legitimacy by drawing on established authors and looking for inspiration in the literary and painting traditions. The historical films were hailed in Australia as national cinema and were received as such internationally.

The image of World War I and the battle of Gallipoli are presented, of course, from a justifiably Australian point of view. "The story . . . gives us back our history. This is what having a film industry is all about," announced a delighted Phillip Adams soon after the film's premiere.[21] But what does *Gallipoli*'s mythic presentation of Australia mean to viewers today? The question is whether the abuse of innocence, as a feature characteristic of Australia, has in our time become anachronistic. By reviving old stereotypes, is *Gallipoli* able to help to create a nation? The answer is partly given in the an approving attitude of the Australian school authorities: The Victorian Education Department produced the film study guide of *Gallipoli* for use in secondary schools.[22]

Anne B. Hutton views the growth of films promoting local history and landscape as a political and economic phenomenon. For her, the decision to promote the outback was a reaction "to the encroachment of American values in urban Australia."[23] Heavily sponsored by the government, the period films produced more sophisticated images of Australia's past, acceptable for the domestic and foreign markets. By stressing the importance of the landscape and the rural virtues of the bushman, the period films offer a different kind of nationalism. They reinforce popular images of Australia earlier elaborated by the representatives of the Heidelberg School.

Weir's *Gallipoli* has been echoed in television miniseries that, though not always dealing with the same period, operate with the same established patterns and reinforce the self-image of Australians. Historical miniseries such as *1915* (1982), *Bodyline* (1984), *Anzacs* (1985), *Vietnam* (1986), and others are sentimental versions of *Gallipoli*. The crowning achievement of this subgenre is Simon Wincer's *The Lighthorsemen* (1987), which even employs Weir's actors, but instead of two friends shows four, for whom the most important thing is "mateship." The outsider, Dave, who has to replace one of them, shares also many similarities with Archy. Although Dave is equipped with almost all bushman attributes, because he is an outsider and a city person, he has to prove in action that he is worth the company of his mates.

Writing on *Gallipoli,* Sylvia Lawson asks the following vital question: "For how much longer must it be assumed that we should identify 'Australia' with images of innocent youth, opposed by repressive Authority and doomed by forces beyond any visible source of control?" (Lawson, 11). Continuing Lawson's argument, one must deduce that the production of innumerable images of youth and innocence, as a feature characteristic for Australia, has become a local speciality. *Gallipoli* presents innocent Australians as characters seemingly satisfied with the fact that they are not English. Perhaps, therefore, this is what being an Australian means? Sydney Nolan puts it as follows: "There is a certain innocence about being an Australian. It is being part of a dream which hasn't been shattered or burnt out."[24]

In this chapter I've discussed *Gallipoli* and its role in the debate on Australian national identity not because Weir's film is unique in its presentation of Australianess but, on the contrary, because it is typical. This film cleverly validates existing stereotypes in order to articulate the Australian national identity. Populist images, reinforcing values

from the bush ("frontier" values), define a national character in contrast to the British one and explore how Australia differs from England within the context of a shared heritage.

Gallipoli and other Australian films of the New Wave period try to reconstruct a continuity between the past and the present to reinforce, rather than to deconstruct, the popular images directly taken from the mythologized past. Commonly projected images of the naive, innocent, "rough but honest" Australian male victimized by the British are repeatedly shown in Australian films. Moreover, Ward's thesis—with its apotheosis of the digger-soldier as the embodiment of Australian psyche—continually serves as a valuable model for the representation of the national type. The bush and the bushman still represent the "real Australia."

The strength of the current image of the Australian national character is its uniqueness and, as a result, the ease with which it can be promoted both within and outside the country. It has only one weakness, yet a significant one—it has little to do with actual present-day Australia.

The inability to come to terms with the real, contemporary Australian identity makes for a peculiar situation. In *Gallipoli* and other Australian films the nostalgic, mythical vision of innocence is presented as "real," a standard against which native Australians can define themselves and viewers overseas can judge them. It may prove the assumption that, being unable to express their uniqueness in any other way, Australians have to apply mythic resolutions.

Peter Weir (bottom left, pointing), Mel Gibson, and Linda Hunt during the filming of *The Year of Living Dangerously* (1982), set in Indonesia during the political disturbances of 1965.

CHAPTER 6

Beyond Shadows:
The Year of Living Dangerously

> Without myth, the spirit starves, and in post-colonial Australia, we are going to build a new myth out of old ones. And I would suggest that these old ones will not belong simply to the European zone, but the Indo-European zone, of which India and Indonesia are both inheritors, as we are.
>
> —C. J. Koch, "Crossing the Gap"

> It's rather a bore to be half something.
>
> —C. J. Koch, *The Year of Living Dangerously*

Since its first appearance in 1978, C. J. Koch's novel *The Year of Living Dangerously* has received a great deal of critical and scholarly attention.[1] Apart from being the winner of the National Book Council Award for Australian literature and the recipient of the Age Book of the Year Award, this novel was also successfully adapted for the screen by Peter Weir, with Koch contributing to the script.

Weir's *The Year of Living Dangerously* (1982) marked a turning point in his career. He has worked in the United States ever since its successful international release. It was also the first Australian film to be fully financed and distributed by a major Hollywood studio, MGM. The film re-creates the political climate of Indonesia in 1965. It deals with a group of Western journalists in Djakarta some months

before and during the unsuccessful PKI (Indonesian Communist Party) coup, which also brought to an end the reign of President Sukarno. Sukarno, the hero of Indonesia's struggles for independence, was overthrown by the right-wing, predominantly Muslim, military establishment headed by General Suharto.

During his reign, Sukarno gave each year a name; from this follows the title of the book and the film. In his Independence Day speech of 17 August 1964 Sukarno called the coming year "the year of living dangerously," in a sense foreseeing the difficulty of managing the country with two radical political forces, the Communists and the Muslims, both trying to overthrow his government.

Certain elements in Koch's novel push the reader down specific interpretative paths. Although realistic in mode, the novel contains a mythological framework that provides a set of possible explanations for the novel's narrative. *The Year of Living Dangerously* is modeled on *wayang kulit,* the Javanese shadow theater. What is even more important, however, is that Indonesia and its culture do not merely serve as an exotic, "Oriental" background for the adventures of the Western reporters/globetrotters/observers. The indigenous Indonesian elements—the puppet theater and the last year of Sukarno's power and his downfall—dominate and structure the work. Furthermore, the Oriental element in *The Year of Living Dangerously* functions as the missing part of Western identity; it is the absent spiritual component of the Occident.

I argue that Susan McKernan is incorrect in stating that, "when Koch writes about India or Indonesia, or even Tasmania [where he was born], he draws out the strongest and most abnormal elements. He is not interested in the day to day life in each place but in the odd, the perverse, the exotic."[2] Although generally praising the novel, McKernan accuses Koch of having a "tourist mentality" because of his presentation of the unknown as both glamorous and threatening. I believe that Indonesia, as presented in *The Year of Living Dangerously,* is neither. Koch provides a rather sympathetic picture of the country where living dangerously has become a norm for both local people and Westerners. This novel effectively deals with materials that, as D. M. Roskies points out, "customarily remain opaque to Western understanding."[3] *The Year of Living Dangerously* certainly is neither an adventure story nor, as McKernan seems to suggest, an exploitation novel aiming to attract readers through the use of "the odd," "the perverse," or "the exotic." Rather, it is a complex novel dealing with Indonesia, which, furthermore, provides a discourse on the nature of

the postcolonial state of mind, on the notion of Australian identity, and on the Australian perception of its Asian neighbors.

Weir's adaptation, with Koch's participation as one of the screen-writers, differs from its literary source in that while the former is politically oriented, the film moves from the political to the melodra-matic within a political setting. Compared with Koch's novel, the film scarcely touches on the complexity of political issues of the East. Instead, it concentrates on Weir's favorite theme of cultural clash: here, East versus West and, more specifically, a Western (Australian) journalist facing social upheaval in a Third World country that he does not really comprehend.

Another important change from novel to film is the choice of nar-rator. In the book, he is a foreign journalist, Cookie; in the film he is replaced by Billy Kwan, who, apart from being the film's narrator, is also a participant and the most powerful figure in the film. Compared with Weir's other filmic characters, Billy Kwan (played by American actress Linda Hunt in an Oscar-winning performance) not only straddles two worlds but also, because of his mixed parentage (Aus-tralian mother, Chinese father), combines elements of both East and West. This factor, and the fact that Billy is played by a woman, adds new meaning to the story: Billy is a mixture of male and female, of East and West, but first and foremost he is a link between these two worlds. He tries to help others overcome their inability to see and understand another culture. Hunt's role in the film is reminiscent of that played by the Aboriginal people in *The Last Wave* (mainly David Gulpilil's Chris). Furthermore, in some respects, the lead character in *The Year of Living Dangerously,* Guy Hamilton (Mel Gibson), an Anglo–Australian journalist newly arrived in Indonesia, in part resembles David Burton from *The Last Wave,* who, though represent-ing the world of reality and Western logic, also tries to understand the "dream" world.

Weir's "generic" culture/nature dichotomy is replaced here with the conflict of Oriental and Occidental. The West is embodied in the Western journalists. Nature finds its equivalent in the East: mysteri-ous and incomprehensible to the outsider. As a rule, Weir is preoccu-pied with the presentation of a middle-class WASP character facing the inexplicable, represented in his films by the Rock, Aborigines, the Amish, and so forth. His central interest lies in presenting the relationship between the two opposing forces (nature and culture, East and West), not in explaining their sources and motifs. Somehow, he always stays on the surface. Weir seems only to need the "other

side" (nature, the East) to show the limitations of his own white Western culture. Talking about *The Year of Living Dangerously*, the director claimed that he "wanted a rather timeless setting in [the] background. The film was about Asia . . . and the background was to reflect that" (Mathews, 105). This is probably the reason that this film, like his others, may be seen as apolitical, romantic, and superficial in its treatment of social issues.

This film is also a part of a larger subgenre that might be called "the adventures of Western journalists in countries experiencing political and economic turmoil." The best-known examples of these films from the 1980s are *Far East* (1982), *Missing* (1982), *Under Fire* (1983), *The Killing Fields* (1984), and *Salvador* (1986).[4]

Whereas some of these films often exploit their exotic setting and concentrate on the misfortunes of the native people, *The Year of Living Dangerously*, in spite of its traditional romantic narrative, contains a strong critique of Western ideology. Carolyn A. Durham writes that "Peter Weir's attack on Western ideology is thorough and relentless to the point of challenging both his own films and certain possibilities of film itself" (Durham 1985b, 117).

Durham's view is particularly relevant in the case of Koch's novel, which goes beyond the usual description of the incomprehensible, mysterious East. Instead of providing a typical critique of Western ideology, Koch concentrates on the opportunities offered by the "Orient" (here Indonesia) and its culture. The Orient is not further "orientalized" by Koch; rather, he attempts to understand and to explain its complexity. In this context, the doppelgänger motif, the motif of the double, extensively employed by Koch and also by Weir, serves to point up not differences but similarities. In Billy Kwan, one of the most extraordinary figures in recent fiction and film, this idea is effectively embodied: he is a man of two worlds/cultures/races, a divided hero of postcolonial reality.

The doubleness, which may be considered a very Australian topic in the context of the country's colonial heritage and its present-day isolation from the rest of the world, is the central metaphor in *The Year of Living Dangerously*. In Weir's film, Asia (Indonesia) does not represent a sinister "otherness" and is not a threat to WASP Australia. The distinction between "us" and "them," Australia and Indonesia, is not clear. Indonesia, the East, the Orient function—as noted earlier—as the missing part of Western identity.

The Year of Living Dangerously introduces "hybrid" personalities, protagonists alienated from their home countries, who have prob-

lems with their personal identities. Both Hamilton and Kwan are dis-
placed persons or, more precisely, men without a center. Hamilton is
certain that Europe is not his world, that he does not belong to the
Northern Hemisphere. Looking at a photograph of Hamilton, Kwan
notices a feature they share: "We are divided men. Your father American, mine Chinese. We are not really certain we are Australian, you
and I. We are not quite at home in the world." Neighboring South-
east Asia offers more to the "rejects" of Europe. To come to terms
with real, not imaginary geography means to overcome the sense of
postcolonial isolation. On the psychological level, Hamilton's and
other journalists' journey into the "otherland" may be interpreted as
a search for the missing part of the self.

Like Koch, Weir tries to go beyond the "Oriental," "exotic," and
"melodramatic" elements of the Indonesian background. To organize
his film as well as to add new meanings, he assimilates the ethos of
wayang kulit into the story. He gives the audience an acceptable set of
explanations by absorbing the notion of *wayang.*

"To understand Java, you'll have to understand the *wayang*," says
Kwan. Teaching Guy to look at the shadows and not at the puppets
while watching a performance, Billy tries to force him to go deeper
into his understanding of the East ("The unseen is all around us, particularly here, in Java"). The *wayang* motif, its Indonesian context, and
the *wayang*'s significance to the narrative aspect of *The Year of Living
Dangerously* is frequently taken up by scholars.[5] Margaret Yong suggests an interesting parallel between the *wayang* puppet theater and
Plato's famous cave.[6] Like the prisoners in the Platonic cave, *wayang*
watchers can also only observe shadows that stand for all real occurrences. To understand reality they must rely on its shadowy images.
This ambiguous, thin delineation between what is perceived as reality and illusion is further developed by Weir in his description of
Western correspondents gathering in the Hotel Indonesia's bar. As
Yong notices, they are also "prisoners inside the dark cave of the
Wayang Bar" (Yong, 29). Ironically, they are voluntary prisoners who
retreat to the illusory shelter of a bar for foreigners in a foreign country.

The motif of puppets is introduced at the beginning of the film:
the *wayang* puppet show appears with the title credits. Later, Billy
introduces the three major figures from the *wayang*: the hero–prince,
the princess, and the dwarf who serves the prince. Billy, who equates
himself with the faithful dwarf, perceives Guy as Prince Arjuna, who
"is a hero, but . . . also . . . fickle and selfish." For Jill Bryant (Sigour-

ney Weaver) he reserves the princess figure, Srikandi, "noble and proud, but headstrong, the princess Arjuna will fall in love with."

The puppet motif is a carefully developed visual metaphor describing both political (President Sukarno) and personal (Billy Kwan) attempts to manipulate the people. The president balances left- and right-wing forces within Indonesia to create the impression of unity between opposites. Kwan idolizes the dictator. For him, Sukarno is successful in his attempts to find an equilibrium between the Marxist revolutionaries and the pressures from the principally Muslim military. Sukarno also stages a performance of the puppet theater for his ministers to covertly make known his will and future political decisions. The shadows stand for reality. Kwan, on the other hand, manipulates and controls other people; he keeps files on everybody he knows, and he is also a kind of accoucheur of the relationship between Hamilton and Jill. The dwarf is introduced in the film right after the credits as he prepares his dossier on Hamilton. Later, sitting in his room at his typewriter, he whispers: "Here, on the printed page, I'm master—just as I am the master in the dark-room, stirring my prints in the magic developing bath. I shuffle like cards the lives I deal with." Both supreme puppet masters (*dalangs*) suffer defeat. Sukarno is replaced after a short but bloody civil war by General Suharto; a disillusioned Kwan encounters death while protesting against Sukarno's policy. Like Billy, Sukarno is a man of dualities: both Hindu and Muslim by birth, a member of the aristocratic class yet a socialist, a charismatic manipulator of the masses and a demagogue, yet, at the same time, a man of considerable merit for Indonesia.

The political aspect of *The Year of Living Dangerously* is stressed throughout, beginning with the film's opening. On his arrival at Djakarta airport, Hamilton is surrounded by anti-imperialist slogans and a hostile crowd of Indonesian poor. "Don't take it personally: you are just a symbol of the West," says Kwan, his guide to the "mysterious Orient." A group of Western journalists, isolated in their hotel and its bar within a hostile and incomprehensible country, deals with the Indonesian people in the manner of President Sukarno, who, in Kwan's words, "uses the people as objects for his pleasure."

Political and sexual exploitation are strictly connected in the film. The representatives of the Western World cannot—or do not want to—overcome their inability to "feel" another culture. The journalists, insensitive to the misery and suffering around them and insensi-

ble to the political nuances of Indonesia and its problems, are interested only in selling their stories. They seem to be satisfied with a
voyeuristic relationship with the natives; they exploit them and
observe their misery. The journalists are introduced to the audience
in terms of their sexual perversions. A British journalist sexually
exploits young boys. An American correspondent spends his stay in
Djakarta in search of sexual pleasure. As Durham points out, "The
camera . . . makes the connection between sexual and colonial
exploitation, between erotic and ideological voyeurism" (Durham
1985b, 121).

In these and many other ways, the film is reminiscent of Weir's earlier works: the incomprehensible East; bad and incompetent Western-
ers/foreigners; an innocent Australian; a cynical Englishman (the
British military attaché, Colonel Henderson, who is portrayed as an
anachronistic symbol of the Empire in the postcolonial world). But
the introduction of the almost mythic Billy Kwan is unusual in that
the dwarf, because of his mixed parentage, combines elements of
both worlds, East and West. Weir is perhaps intentionally ironic in
portraying Kwan, the strongest character in the film, as a dwarf. In
Weir's adaptation Kwan is the narrator and moral center of the film.
Played by Hunt, Kwan is Eastern and Western, male and female,
detached observer and passionate participant.[7]

The tormented Australian-Chinese cameraman, who is the link
between the two worlds, tries to understand and to help the Indonesians as much as he can. He repeatedly borrows a phrase from Luke,
later used by Leo Tolstoy: "What then must we do?" He poses the
same question in an emotional climax as his world rapidly disinte-
grates. After learning of the death of his adopted child and having
seen groups of starving Indonesians fighting for rice, Kwan, with
photographs of local faces all around him, cries and passionately types
this very question on his typewriter. The poignant third song—"On
Going to Sleep"—from Richard Strauss's "Four Last Songs" emphasizes his desperate search for a solution. Kwan finds it in another
small attempt to change the reality around him; his unsuccessful
struggle to attract Sukarno's attention by hanging a banner reading
"Sukarno, feed your people," from a window results in his tragic
death at the hands of the security forces.

According to Durham, the relationship between vision and
knowledge is the key to the meaning of the film. For her, this subver-
sive, self-reflexive film "centres its critique on the conception and the
function of vision" (Durham 1985b, 120). The Australian reporter,

likely because of his youth and innocence, represents hope for Kwan: he brings the possibility of learning to see and feel in a new light. As a cameraman, Kwan is not only Hamilton's eyes ("I can be your eyes," he says) but also his "architect of images," combining the seeing of things with feeling them. Kwan devotes all his energy to teaching Guy to see (understood as "feel") the true Indonesia, which is not very far from the *Wayang* bar. Losing Kwan, Hamilton loses his only chance to comprehend the Eastern World around him. The protagonist's inability to "feel" the real Indonesia is literally presented in the final sequences of the film as his partial blindness. Hamilton's loss of vision (from a detached retina) serves as a metaphor for the West's lack of "vision," its inability to comprehend occurrences unrelated to its own cultural assumptions. In the film's final sequence, Hamilton's Indonesian assistant, Kumar (Bembol Roco), a member of the Communist Party, puts it this way: "Billy Kwan was right. Westerners don't have answers anymore."

This film's main concern is the concept of the "mysterious Orient," which is beyond Western comprehension. In this context, the question introduced by James Roy MacBean in the subtitle of his article "Watching the Third World Watchers"—"Mysterious Orient or, Merely the Insensitive Western Observer?"—is of crucial importance (MacBean, 8). Another important aspect of the film is the voyeurism of Kwan and the foreign correspondents. As compared with the exploitive journalists, Billy Kwan is the more complex voyeur. Because of his inconspicuous appearance, he chooses a handsome alter ego (a double) in Hamilton and thereby embellishes his image. When Kwan is convinced that his doppelgänger is equipped with all of his virtues, he introduces Hamilton to Jill, a secretary from the British Embassy, with whom Kwan is in love. When Billy realizes that she does not love him, the dwarf promotes his "substitute" and gets pleasure from being close to the lovers. Then, he controls their actions, offers his flat to them, spies on them, photographs them, and adds to his dossiers on them. Moreover, when the romance becomes a source of disappointment for him, he tries to put an end to it. "I believed in you," Kwan tells Hamilton, "I made you see things, I made you feel something about what you write, I gave you my trust, so did Jill . . . I created you!"

At first glance, Hamilton and Kwan seem an unlikely pair: a physically attractive, eager Anglo-Australian journalist and a tragicomic, megalomaniac Chinese-Australian dwarf. But as Kwan says, they

Mel Gibson (Guy Hamilton) and Sigourney Weaver (Jill Bryant) as lovers in *The Year of Living Dangerously* (1982).

"make a great team . . . you for the words, me for the pictures. I can be your eyes." Both Hamilton and Kwan are "incomplete human beings": they have to rely on and supplement each other. On the one hand, Hamilton is an "object of desire" and worship for Kwan, on the other, an object of manipulation and re-creation. Jill touches on the true motif of Billy's actions when she notes that Hamilton is "everything [Billy] wants to be." Kwan makes efforts to subordinate and shape Hamilton. Nonetheless, as in Gothic novels and horror films dealing with the relationship between the creator and the creature/monster (the Frankenstein motif), the creature becomes a source of disappointment for the creator, who inevitably cannot completely control his creation.

Kwan's character combines both voyeuristic and puppet-master elements. When the puppets gradually slip out of his hands, his role (like that of President Sukarno) ends. Kwan has carefully engineered relationships with others (Sukarno; an Indonesian woman, Ibu, with a child he supports; Hamilton) and between others (Hamilton and

Jill); nonetheless, this construction collapses. Like Sukarno, Kwan cannot control his creation: the puppets he once controlled slip out of his manipulative grasp to take on lives of their own. A puppeteer without his puppets is a figure of no importance, a master without slaves, a Dr. Frankenstein without his laboratory. The tragic death of Kwan serves to emphasize this moment of helplessness.

The Year of Living Dangerously is Kwan's film, and his presence adds an important dimension to it. The film begins with Kwan and his voiceover comments introducing Hamilton; the audience then sees most of the events from his point of view. His voice-over narration infuses the film with a dreamlike mood. Kwan's death marks the real end of the film. When Kwan is no longer on screen, *The Year of Living Dangerously* rapidly lapses into a clichéd Hollywood film.

For the first time in his career Weir employs in *The Year of Living Dangerously* the motif of romantic love, which he also presents in his next film, *Witness*. Interestingly, Jill and Hamilton's romance, though it seems to dominate the film, is less important than Guy's relationship with his "creator," Kwan. In presenting and developing the romance, Weir is conventional. Both lovers look as if taken from an American dream: they are handsome, independent, ambitious individuals surrounded by the exotic and impoverished masses. Some sequences are familiar from hundreds of films (their eyes meeting across the room; the happy ending—reunion and embrace), and Weir does nothing to modify these adopted images. On the contrary, as in his earlier films, the director does not attach much importance to "the story." For Weir, "the story" is always only a pretext through which to present ideas, and he does not even try to mask his intentions. He easily employs recognizable, only intensified images to fix audience attention on ideas.

The oneiric aspect of the film is achieved through consciously employed visual images. Russell Boyd's photography captures the tropical, beautiful, but hostile Indonesia. The characters move in this dreamlike landscape as if driven by an invisible force. Some sequences possess a nightmarish quality. The best examples of this are the shots of Djakarta when Guy arrives on his first foreign assignment, the images of poverty-stricken Indonesians, the bloody military coup and Guy's desperate drive to the airport, shots of mist rising off the canals, the slums of Djakarta, and a tropical downpour. Moreover, Weir also employs a "real" nightmare, Hamilton's troubled dream of drowning, which, incidentally, plays on the familiar Weirian

water motif. Frequent shots through the windshield of Hamilton's car help to create a hallucinatory atmosphere. Oneiricism is enhanced by the use of shadows, which also call to mind the puppet motif. They appear at the beginning of the film, then during the love scene (the shadow of kissing lovers), and when Hamilton broadcasts his first report (a silhouetted shadow on the window). Maurice Jarre's music plays an important role in generating this dreamlike mood; its tone mainly stresses the romantic.

In his first four feature films (*Picnic at Hanging Rock* once again being the best example), Weir "discourages" the spectator from following the story. *Gallipoli* and, especially, *The Year of Living Dangerously*, in spite of their more linear narrative lines, only appear to work differently. By presenting an easy-to-follow plot, Weir concentrates on creating an unusual mood and on exploring themes interesting to him, this time not hidden in the narrative line but rather apparent, even obvious. It is possible to say that since *Gallipoli* Weir has changed his method of presenting a story, but this does not mean he has changed the content. For some critics, *The Year of Living Dangerously* is the pinnacle of Weir's earlier works.[8] He successfully employs a conventional narrative structure and yet is able to infuse it with a recognizable personal style.

CHAPTER 7

Witness in the Amish Land

A culture can only represent itself to itself (i.e., consciously acknowledge its own choices) in relation to the contrasting practices of another culture. Looking at others is the only way we become able to speak.

—John P. McGowan, "Looking at the (Alter)natives: Peter Weir's *Witness*"

Peter Weir's first film set entirely within American filmic and American cultural context, *Witness* (1985), brought him eight Academy Award nominations, including his first for best director. The film won two Academy Awards, one for best original screenplay (by Earl K. Wallace and Pamela Wallace) and one for best editing (by Thom Noble). *Witness* is also Weir's major box-office and critical success, generally praised for its ability to combine the traditional American narrative formula with his unique approach to filmmaking.[1]

Witness presents another cross-cultural hero, a Philadelphia police captain, John Book (Harrison Ford), forced by occurrences beyond his control to witness the practices of another culture, that of the American Amish. The collision of two separate worlds, the violent urban world of Book and the rural pacifist microcosm of the Amish, is the core of this film. It is this interaction of individuals from two different cultures or backgrounds, the theme of contrasted ways of life, that is the customary focus in Weir's films. The protagonist of *Witness* in many respects resembles the heroes of Weir's previous works, chiefly David Burton of *The Last Wave*. In *The Last Wave* and in *Witness,* the viewer explores the Aboriginal and Amish cultures,

respectively, not from the inside but through a mediator from his or her own culture. As Richard Combs observes, the dreamtime of the Aborigines is replaced in *Witness* by the dream life of the Amish—a life out of time.[2] In this sense, *Witness* can almost be taken as *The Last Wave* in an American context.[3]

Witness can also be described as a romantic thriller, a variation on the standard American genre in an unusual rural setting. It can also be argued that *Witness* is, in fact, a redesigned western. Nonetheless, as in his other films, Weir does not make a traditional film with a conventional plot. *Witness* is a cross-generic film that employs elements of the western, the police thriller, and the romance. It is a perfectly executed mainstream film that nonetheless clearly bears the director's personal stamp.

Despite the artistic constraints of big American studio productions, Weir's personal touch is evident from the first scene. The open-

Harrison Ford, as Philadelphia police detective John Book, observes Lucas Haas (Samuel Lapp) as the Amish boy tries to identify a murder suspect in *Witness* (1985).

ing sequence of *Witness* introduces the Amish and their gentle and anachronistic rhythm of life. In the first pastoral scene, the dark-clothed Amish emerge from an oceanlike field of green crops. The image is dominated by the waving grass as the Amish, some walking, some in their buggies, move in an unknown direction. Then, in a long shot the camera reveals a small Amish settlement situated amid the "ocean of grass." The title "Pennsylvania, 1984," appears on the screen, superimposed over the Amish on their way to the settlement; the date likely surprises the viewer, who has been prepared by the visuals for a historical-pastoral film set in the nineteenth century. Weir opens *Picnic at Hanging Rock* and *The Last Wave* with a series of similarly well-composed shots. *Witness,* however, is less atmospheric and, to a large extent, relies on linear narrative strengthened by the use of haunting images. From the first scene *Witness* is a well-balanced combination of straightforward, well-written screenplay and pure visuals: Weir turns an articulate Hollywood script into a recognizably personal work of art.

In the second scene, a collection of close-ups of the Amish attending the funeral of the husband of Rachel Lapp (Kelly McGillis) introduces the viewer to a community ruled by its own laws and traditions. The absence of English in the first scenes (only High German is used, as always in Amish religious gatherings) emphasizes the uniqueness of the observed community; it is also stressed by the plainness and uniformity of the clothing people wear. These opening images, reinforced by Maurice Jarre's ethereal score, show the Amish in their natural, wide-open setting and present a strong sense of community values. The next sequence, consisting of four shots, purely visual and without dialogue, focuses on reinforcing characteristics already introduced. It shows people working in the field according to the rhythm of the sun: employing Jarre's refined score and dissolves between shots, Weir suggests the otherworldly qualities of the community and its allegiance to the land.

After this brief introduction to the Amish pastoral life, the action moves rapidly to an urban setting. On her way to Baltimore, while waiting for a train in Philadelphia, the recently widowed Rachel and her eight-year-old son, Samuel (Lukas Haas), experience the brutality of the outside world. "You be careful out among them English," is the warning given to Rachel by her father-in-law, Eli Lapp (Jan Rubes), before she leaves the peaceful Amish community. His premonition is fully materialized. The brutal murder of an undercover narcotics officer is witnessed by Samuel, who remains unseen by the

murderer, setting off a chain of events that allows the director to bring together two different cultures and to then contrast their different ways of life. Police detective Book has to deal with the case and, with the help of Samuel, discovers that those behind the murder are corrupt cops, including his department chief and friend, Deputy Commissioner Schaeffer (Josef Sommer). Book, wounded by another cop, McFee (Danny Glover), and fearing for the safety of Samuel, is forced to escape the corruption of his world and to seek refuge in the Amish community.

This unusual situation, which enables the protagonist to penetrate a different world, is often employed by Weir. As early as in his first feature film, *The Cars That Ate Paris,* Weir developed a similar idea: the hero (Arthur Waldo), clashing with a different, nightmarish world in which he is forced to stay, is also a participant in/observer of an unusual community. Like Waldo, Book involuntarily places himself in the hands of a different community. Because of the need to keep his and the boy's identity secret ("If they find me, they find the boy"), the police detective cannot be taken to the hospital. There is, however, one indispensable difference between the two protagonists: Book, a representative of the violent outside world, brings violence to the Amish and his presence among them poses a constant threat to the community; Waldo's presence among the grotesquely depraved community of Paris puts only Waldo in jeopardy.

A similar narrative endeavor, in which the protagonist is placed in an alien environment beyond his comprehension (or his will to comprehend) is employed by Weir most noticeably in *The Last Wave,* where another representative of the law has an opportunity to meet a different culture. *Witness* shares its "ethnographic" interest in another culture with *The Year of Living Dangerously.* The protagonists of these two films, in spite of the encouragement from others (Billy Kwan, Rachel Lapp), choose a "touristy" approach to the strange environment. No wonder then that in both films separate worlds cannot merge and the boundaries between them cannot be crossed. As is the case with the majority of Peter Weir's films, *Witness* is built on distinct polarities, namely:

> The Amish versus mainstream Americans
> An archaic way of life versus the modern way of life
> Country versus city
> A nonviolent world versus a violent world
> Harmony versus alienation

Innocence versus aggression
Insiders versus outsiders

Witness centers on the conflict of cultures. Weir constantly employs the otherness of the Amish and opposes their values and way of life in preference for those of the "civilized" world.

Descendants of Swiss Anabaptists who are named after their leader, Jacob Ammann, the Amish settled in Pennsylvania in 1727.[4] They are mainly farmers and artisans who, throughout the ages, have managed to remain secluded from the rest of the world for religious reasons. The Amish differ not only in their way of thinking but also in appearance. They continue to dress as their ancestors did, they reject much of modern technology, and their use of a dialect of the German language, which is generally described as Pennsylvania German or Pennsylvania Dutch, sets them apart from the outside world. The uncorrupt, straightforward nature of the Amish is also emphasized in *Witness* by the directness of their speech, which sometimes creates humorous situations. ("We are happy you are going to live,

Peter Weir (left) on location in Pennsylvania Dutch country for *Witness* (1985), with Kelly McGillis (Rachel Lapp), Jan Rubes (Rachel's father-in-law, Eli), and Harrison Ford (John Book).

John Book," says Rachel. "We didn't know what we should do if you died.")

The conflict between the attractive agrarian way of life and the dangers of urban living organizes the film. The inhospitable city is contrasted with the cozy familiarity of the village. Leaving the safety of their community, Rachel and Lucas find themselves in a world with different rules. The Amish in Philadelphia are in an alien and threatening "world of English." The first part of the film, in which the Amish community is introduced, prepares the viewer for the sharp contrast in the Philadelphia sequence. The search for the suspect in a tough neighborhood sets up a distinct contrast between the idealized rural world and the hostile and dangerous urban environment by showing violence, which is unacceptable among the Amish. Rachel stresses this contrast by protesting: "We want nothing to do with your laws."

The irreconcilability of the two cultures is shown in the scene in which Schaeffer makes a phone call to a Lancaster police sergeant in an effort to track down Book. Methods customary in an urban environment are useless in the Amish community, where the Lapp surname is widespread. Schaeffer then suggests to the sergeant that he "do some telephoning." "Yes, maybe I could," responds the sergeant. "But since the Amish don't have any telephones, I wouldn't know whom to call." "Thank you, sergeant. It's been an education," says Schaeffer, giving up.

Witness can also be taken as a meditation on violence, on what happens to nonviolent behavior in the face of violent assault. The film is framed by violent action sequences, and in the middle section simultaneously develops themes of love and violence. In his close reading of *Witness,* Wayne J. McMullen asserts that the Amish are portrayed as an attractive alternative to the violent urban life. He states that the ideological project of Weir's film is not only to acknowledge the attractions of a rural and pacifist lifestyle, but simultaneously, not to force the viewer to make choices between two incompatible ways of life: materialistic/violent and pacifist/agrarian.[5] In his perceptive study, McMullen focuses on this juxtaposition of agrarian and urban values and lifestyles but also on the methods employed by the director to invite the viewer to participate in the film's vision of Amish society. McMullen's penetrating scene-by-scene analysis shows Weir's consistency in building our sympathy for the values represented by the Amish.

The viewer feels sympathy for but does not identify with the Amish. Among other things, as John P. McGowan points out, the Sam Cooke song "What a Wonderful World" helps viewers to recognize the huge gap separating them from the Amish;[6] it seems strange that such a familiar, well-liked song would be perceived by the Amish— here in the person of Rachel's father-in-law, Eli—as corrupting or sinful. The "utopian" aspect of Amish life is therefore interesting but not tempting for the viewer, alternative but not acceptable. "If Amish life is utopian," states McGowan, "it is utopia forged by renunciation, a utopia unattractive in precisely the same ways that More's Utopia chills modern readers" (McGowan, 43).[7]

The viewer, although appreciative of the peaceful lifestyle of the Amish, is likely ready to support violent action executed by Book. In the context of *Witness,* Book's violence is justifiable, the only way to survive in a violent world. In many aspects Book acts like a lonely avenger from the series of films concerning "prosocial" aggression— that is, intended to protect society. Clint Eastwood's *Dirty Harry* (1971), Charles Bronson's *Death Wish* (1974), and their sequels and countless imitations present heroes who, surrounded by violence and corruption, adopt violent methods themselves as the only apparent means to restore normality. The violence of these protagonists equals and sometimes surpasses that of the villains, though their goal is always a "noble" one—eradicating violence by literally eliminating its source.

John Book is given only this choice in the film, and he acts on it with the viewer's understanding and support.[8] After learning of his partner's death from a pay phone—his only means of contact with his old life—("killed in the line of duty" is the official version but the viewer knows that Schaeffer is behind it), Book reacts violently against the rednecks who harass the Amish as they travel by horse and buggy on their way back to their community. By this act, he not only shows his frustration but also proves to the Amish that he has not assimilated their beliefs: "This is not our way," says Eli. "But this is my way," responds Book. Aggression is met with aggression. The first part of this scene prepares the viewer to accept it as a necessary behavior later in the film.

Detective Book also finds himself in a situation typical for Weir's protagonists. In conflict with a different, closed culture, he questions his own values. The growing attraction between him and Rachel is suddenly interrupted when the outer world violently intrudes on Amish territory, disrupting their serene way of life. A similar situation

occurs in Weir's next film, *The Mosquito Coast,* in which Fox's idyll in the jungle ends with the appearance of the mysterious bandits.[9]

The unreconcilable nature of the Amish world and the English world is shown most clearly in the scene in which Samuel plays with Book's revolver. Book tries to teach the boy about the danger of a loaded gun, while Samuel's mother and grandfather present the Amish point of view on violence. "What you take into your hands, you take into your heart," states Eli, presenting a glimpse of Amish pacifism. The intruding world of the English, however, forces Book to choose "his way." In the scene in which Rachel and Book dance to Cooke's "Wonderful World," the outraged Eli blames Rachel for bringing violence to the community, in a sense foretelling the final sequence of the film: "Rachel, you bring this man to our house. With his gun of the hand. You bring fear to this house. Fear of English with guns coming after."

Its polemics on violence, which is in itself a very American topic, places this film in the broader tradition of the Hollywood cinema. One of the most obvious and well-known examples is Fred Zinnemann's *High Noon* (1952), in which a Quaker woman (Grace Kelly) stands behind "her man" and acts against her own and her community's principles. Her husband-sheriff (Gary Cooper), deserted by friends, prepares himself for a deadly fight with the criminal avenger returning to the town on the noon train. In a decisive final scene, the sheriff's wife saves his life by shooting one of the aggressors from behind.

In her essay on the image of nonviolence in *Witness* and earlier films such as *Sergeant York* (1941, Howard Hawks) and *Friendly Persuasion* (1956, William Wyler), Linda Hansen discusses a tradition in American cinema in which heroes try to avoid violence but are finally forced to accept it and defend themselves, their families, or their country by being even more violent than their attackers. Considering this tradition, Hansen says that it is reasonable to expect Rachel to act like the Quaker woman in *High Noon*.[10] But Weir does not follow this path, which is also a recurrent motif in some contemporary action films in which a heroine, usually a mother/wife figure, shoots the aggressor in the final scene, acting not only to protect her loved one(s) but also the integrity of her family. *Fatal Attraction* (Adrian Lyne, 1987) and *Someone to Watch Over Me* (Ridley Scott, 1988) serve as good examples of this convention. Instead of following this course, *Witness* ends with a show of the community's strength, of its ability to overpower the armed aggressor in a nonviolent way.

There is a deliberate evocation of the western genre in *Witness* in a scene in which the corrupt policemen suddenly enter the Amish land. In a shot typical to the Western (figures framed from behind, Seale's camera shows their legs and guns in their hands), Weir announces the forthcoming duel. Dressed in professional-looking suits, the villains invade the nonviolent enclave. They are, however, outmaneuvered by Book and the Amish, who stand silently but firmly behind him ("acting by not acting").

John Book belongs to a long list of characters inseparably linked with Hollywood mythology: the urban policeman/hero, smart, clean, uncorrupted, and straightforward. As a standard cop, he is single ("afraid of the responsibility," Rachel recalls his sister, Elaine, saying). Typically, his work partner seems to be more important to him than women. Rachel's comment to Book after her conversation with his sister describes his motives in the following way: "You like policing because you think you are right about everything. And you are the only one who can do anything." Schaeffer, when confronting Book's partner, Carter, points out that both the police and the Amish are "cults or clubs with their own rules." Both Book and Rachel break the rules of their "cults": Book by turning against his (corrupt) superiors, Rachel by being attracted to a man from outside her community.

The clash of cultures, values, and attitudes is once again more important for the director than a detailed examination of different cultures. Weir's nostalgic view of Amish life (another romanticization of a "primitive" culture, this time an archaic rural culture) does not introduce new elements into our knowledge of the Amish community. His ethnographic observations serve only to emphasize the difference between "the modern" and "the archaic" and to show the viewer people acting in both realms. The romance between two people from different cultures makes for an opportunity to bring those cultures together. But the differences are insurmountable on both sides. The ending of *Witness* is characteristic for Weir: the two cultures cannot merge. Book has to return to his world, leaving Rachel behind in the community to which she belongs.

In leaving the Amish community, Book enables Rachel's Amish suitor, Daniel Hochleitner (Alexander Godunov), to win her over. In the last scene, Daniel, who from the film's beginning demonstrates a romantic interest in Rachel, walks victoriously toward the Lapp farm. Earlier, during the barn-raising scene, tension emerges between Hochleitner and Book; to the disapproval of the community, Rachel

Kelly McGillis (Rachel Lapp), shows her favor for "outsider" Harrison Ford (John Book) by serving him before she does her would-be Amish suitor, Alexander Godunov (Daniel Hochleitner), who looks on. From *Witness* (1985).

favors Book by serving him first. The threat of her being shunned is articulated by Eli: "Do you know what it means?" he asks. "I cannot sit at table with you. I cannot take a thing from your hand. I cannot go to worship with you." The sensual, vulnerable Rachel communicates to Book her desire for physical intimacy, but he declines her unspoken offer. "If we would have made love last night," he states the next day, "I would have to stay or you have to leave." As in some of Weir's earlier films (such as *Gallipoli* and *The Year of Living Dangerously*), Weir is interested in the personal dimension of the conflict. The conflict between the dominant culture and a minority culture is brought to light through a romance, which broaches the boundaries of the two cultures. The unfulfilled romance between Rachel and Book and the sexual tension between them occupies Weir more than the examination of the cultural clash.

The title of the film refers not only to the Amish boy, Samuel (his innocent gaze is often employed by Weir), but—perhaps most of

all—to John Book. There are, in fact, two witnesses in the film: Samuel, who observes the alien world of the English, and Book, who witnesses the anachronistic life of the Amish. Both cultures look at each other through their representatives. The innocent gaze of the boy is juxtaposed with the "conscious" look of the policeman. Weir employs a subjective camera technique to enhance the identification with the Amish. The first part of the film, and especially the Philadelphia sequence, is shown from Samuel's point of view. The viewer shares his amazement ("You'll see so many things," says Hochleitner) in the scenes preceding the murder and then his horror afterward. Weir employs many low-angle shots to emphasize the boy's perspective. The frame composition in the scene in which Samuel explores the train station is filled with visual stimuli experienced by Samuel: "normally" dressed people, a water fountain, a Hasidic Jew whom the boy takes for an Amish, a large statue with an angel.

The innocent gaze of the boy is brutally interrupted by the invasion of violence from the outside world: the viewer experiences Samuel's terror while witnessing the scene alien to his world. Shown mostly from his point of view, the murder scene heightens the emotional impact on the viewer. Another scene shown from Samuel's perspective (both physical and psychological) is the identification of the killer as the police inspector, McFee. In this particular scene, intensified by Jarre's music, Weir employs his characteristic visual style. A slow zoom toward McFee's photo, displayed to honor his achievements as a policeman, signals the boy's moment of discovery. Then, Weir cross-cuts close-ups of Samuel and Book. When Book catches Samuel's glance, he moves in slow motion toward the boy. The whole scene, filmed in an unreal, slow-motion speed, bears a strong resemblance to several scenes from Weir's *Picnic at Hanging Rock* (for instance, the girls' ascent toward the rock).

After Samuel points out McFee, his perspective is no longer needed. His central position is taken over by Book and the romance between him and Rachel. As the action moves once again to the rural setting, the perspective of the policeman becomes the dominant one. Through his eyes the viewer discovers the Amish way of life.

The cinematography by John Seale emphasizes the communal aspect of the Amish community and its link with the land. In the establishing shot, the Amish are presented as a part of the natural landscape. To accentuate interaction between characters, the camera focuses on facial expressions. Frequent close-ups and telephoto shots fill the screen. There is, however, a difference in the way the Amish

and the representatives of the urban world are portrayed. The camera deliberately creates the otherworldly qualities of the Amish: framing, soft lighting (the light of lanterns), and editing contribute to this impression. The images of the Amish are reminiscent of the great Flemish painters. In an interview done after the film, Weir acknowledges the influence of an exhibition of Dutch paintings called "Dutch Masters" that opened in Philadelphia during the filming of *Witness*.[11] Vermeer's paintings are a source of inspiration for many shots, as in the scene in which Book is healed by the Amish and nursed by Rachel. This unworldly look is reserved for the Amish; the city dwellers, including Book, are portrayed in a "realistic" fashion. Maurice Jarre's score stresses mainly the ethereality of the Amish community and plays an important role in creating a dated atmosphere. Together with Seale's cinematography, it emphasizes the innocence of the Amish in contrast with the corruption and aggression of the urban culture.

Some of the scenes in *Witness,* employed to emphasize the pastoral life of the Amish, approach cliché and resemble the style of television commercials. The barn-building sequence, for instance, an idyllic, Disneyesque scene, consists of shots of antlike activities, harmony, labor division by gender (men building, women and children assisting). The motif of romantic love and the characterization of the saintlike Amish are equally obviously portrayed. Weir, however, seems to be aware of the banality of some of these images. Moreover, he intensifies and comments on them; for instance, when Book and Rachel dance together to music forbidden to her (Sam Cooke's "What a Wonderful World") or when Book mimics a television commercial ("Honey, that's great coffee!").

An easy-to-follow narrative line and familiar images from many films, which are magnified by Weir, serve as means for building a peculiar mood. As in his earlier works, Weir's method of presenting the story is subordinated to specific themes, ever-present in his films. Thematics contribute to oneiricism. However, if in his earliest works Weir builds themes through contiguity—small observations grouped in an impressionistic fashion—now he does so by introducing causality and a strong, fluent narrative line.

Commenting on the barn-raising scene, Wayne McMullen emphasizes its "mosaic-like style of editing," characterized by the fact that almost all the shots, which look like portraits in themselves, contribute to a general effect of wholeness (McMullen, 219–20). Although the visual style of *Witness* undoubtedly sanctions

McMullen's assertion, it is rather Weir's early films that most exemplify this characteristic. *Picnic at Hanging Rock,* in particular, is not only a collection of impressionistic images; its very method of editing resembles an impressionist painting—lacking typical linear narration, the film achieves wholeness through the association and interaction of all the constituent elements.

Another important feature of Weir's style in *Witness* is the insignificance of dialogue. The themes are developed in purely visual terms. The Amish, excluding Eli's patriarchal comments, do not present their views verbally. The romance between Rachel and Book also develops without words. The impact of this film is achieved by cinematography and editing alone. McGowan believes, however, that the absence of dialogue, which advances the plot, limits the viewer to a touristy experience. "What is striking about *Witness,*" he remarks, "is how completely its own encounter is limited to looking, which is keeping with film's dominant emphasis on the visual, but which does seem to condemn us to a certain superficiality" (McGowan, 41).

On one hand, McGowan asserts, Weir reveals a certain "delicacy" in not wanting to intrude "too far." On the other, by allowing viewers only limited access to another culture, he makes it difficult for them to understand it; we always require "words of negation."[12] Weir does not repeat the mistake he made in *The Last Wave,* in which he could not abstain from naming things or from being too literal. In *Witness* he avoids explicit dialogue and keeps commentary to a minimum. He does so not because the Amish have little to say about themselves but because it is said in purely visual terms.

CHAPTER 8

Jungle Utopia in *The Mosquito Coast*

Nobody loves America more than I do. That's why I left.
— Allie Fox in *The Mosquito Coast*

Paul Theroux's novel *The Mosquito Coast*,[1] which has been described
as his "finest imaginative fiction,"[2] attracted film producers since the
time of its appearance in 1982. Jerome Hellman, producer of *Midnight Cowboy* (1969) and *Coming Home* (1978), purchased the film
rights and committed himself to bringing the story to the screen,
engaging Paul Schrader to write a screenplay. As he did in writing
the screenplays for *Taxi Driver* (1976) and *Raging Bull* (1980),
Schrader emphasized the maniacal aspect of the protagonist's character. The same people who made the successful *Witness* reunited to
adapt Theroux's popular novel: editor Thom Noble, cinematographer
John Seale, leading actor Harrison Ford, and composer Maurice
Jarre. In spite of this mutual effort, however, *The Mosquito Coast*
(1986) met with only limited critical and box-office success.

The main character of *The Mosquito Coast,* an eccentric genius-
inventor, Allie Fox (Harrison Ford), is disenchanted with the United
States and decides to immigrate with his family to the Mosquito
Coast of Central America, to begin civilization anew in a small forgotten place called Jeronimo. Fox's quest for paradise, however,
changes into a desperate fight for survival. Madly pursuing his unfulfilled dream of colonizing the new land, Allie loses his mind and his
life.

Schrader's screenplay is a faithful adaptation (not an interpretation) of Theroux's novel. Nevertheless, in calling Weir's film a "textbook example of the dangers of literary adaptation," Terrence Rafferty rightly states that "by stripping the novel of its dense verbal texture, Schrader and Weir draw attention to the thinness of the story, bringing all its flaws to light: the sketchy, indifferent characterizations of the younger Fox children, the natives of the Mosquito Coast and, especially, Allie's long-suffering wife; the lack of surprise or tension in the action scenes; the essential monotony of the conception."[3]

These factors certainly contributed to this film's less-than-warm critical reception. Although Weir's film is a faithful adaptation, it misses the spirit of the novel. As in Theroux's novel, Weir's film focuses on Allie Fox (valiantly played by Ford), who in Weir's version is a more sympathetic and therefore a more tragic figure than in the novel. Allie's oldest son, thirteen-year-old Charlie (River Phoenix), the voice-over narrator of the film as well as the narrator of the novel, plays a less active role in the film. Everything and everybody is subordinated to the main character; his family is without any clear thematic role in the film as evidenced by Fox's submissive, unnamed (as she is in the novel) wife—"Mother" (Helen Mirren).

As in the novel, the role of the black characters in Weir's film is of secondary importance. With the exception of the Creole boatman, Mr. Haddy (Conrad Roberts), their portrayal is one-dimensional and stereotypical. Haddy not only ferries the Fox family to their new jungle home but also remains faithful to them and appears in key moments throughout the narrative. Later, even he is perceived by Fox as a threat to his absolute power over his family: his confrontation with Allie is presented in the fashion of a Western duel. Anyone whose opinion differs from that of Fox finds himself in conflict with the protagonist. Like the Reverend Mr. Spellgood (André Gregory), a missionary who commutes between his two churches, a drive-in in Baltimore and a mission on the Mosquito Coast, Fox needs no partners, only followers, to fulfil his vision. The Jeronimo villagers are presented as submissive, obedient, voiceless, and, consequently, likeable figures. Like Allie's family, they have no thematic role to play: they are part of the exotic landscape, passive objects of the white man's colonial experiments. As Rafferty suggests, the individuals are "premises rather than characters" (Rafferty, 684). A similar objection is raised by Stanley Kauffmann, for whom the viewer of The Mosquito Coast gets only a "silhouette, proportionate but unrealized."[4]

Harrison Ford as inventor Allie Fox, obsessed with building a jungle utopia, in *The Mosquito Coast* (1986).

According to Steven R. Luebke, Theroux's novel belongs to the homesteading narratives that repeat the story of the Pilgrim migration to America.[5] These narratives deal with the quest to establish a society free of corruption, a new social order in a new land. In opposition to the traditional homesteading stories, *The Mosquito Coast* begins in Massachusetts (the Pilgrims' destination) and moves to Central America. Luebke points out that the predominant trend in recent homesteading narratives is to invert the traditional formula (Luebke, 228). This inversion is intended as a means of critique of contemporary society. To accomplish his dream, the protagonist has to look for a new place beyond that founded by the Pilgrims and other immigrants, a place beyond the United States. Contrary to its older counterpart, the contemporary homesteading journey is pessimistic and without positive solutions. The protagonist's journey usually ends in a disaster: he is unable to build an alternative society, for he is entangled in situations ironically echoing his experiences in his home country.

Several features contribute to the perception of Weir's *The Mosquito Coast* as a homesteading narrative. The protagonist possesses a

passionate pioneering spirit and a desire for change. America no longer offers him an opportunity to show this side of himself. "I just work here—that's the attitude," he tells his son after a visit to the local hardware store. For Allie Fox, this is the source of the country's downfall. "Starting from scratch. . . . This is what I've always dreamt about," he declares. The maverick inventor ("nine patents, six pending") and Harvard dropout (Charlie states proudly that his father left Harvard "to get an education") is driven by an unspent energy, an urge to change, a sense of mission. His desire is to bring civilization to the wilderness, as did the Pilgrim Fathers before him.

Fox's pioneering, antiauthoritarian, unstoppable spirit has to find a new land to tame and to shape according to his own vision. He has to build his own Garden of Eden. He takes his family—wife, two teenage sons, and twin girls—to a jungle village, escaping to an idyllic paradise that offers him a chance to fulfill his pioneering dream: to bring civilization (but without its negative aspects) to the natives of the Mosquito Coast. In Jeronimo, the family celebrates a Thanksgiving meal after finishing the first stage of the settlement. Shortly thereafter, Fox's selfishness, which is the essential driving force of his actions, becomes more visible.

Fox's desire is to build a utopia, a paradise in which a happier (perfect by definition) kind of life can be lived. However, utopia (also by definition) is a nonexistent place; the word comes from the Greek: *ou* meaning no, *topos* meaning place. *Utopia* is generally defined as a place that does not exist, a place of ideal proportion, the end product of some impractical scheme for improving the world. Fox's vision is carried out to its extremely undesirable conclusion: utopia turns to dystopia. The more utopia becomes itself, the more it becomes its opposite. The ignorant pursuit of illusory progress is the founder of most dystopias. George Orwell's *1984,* Aldous Huxley's *Brave New World* (1932), and Kurt Vonnegut's *Player Piano* (1952) debunk the utopian dream of a golden age in which technology elevates the quality of life.

Another important reason for Fox's flight into the jungle is his obsession with the idea that civil war and nuclear annihilation are coming. After the destruction of Jeronimo, Allie tells his family that the United States has been destroyed, as he predicted, in a nuclear holocaust, thereby justifying his subsequent actions. He sees himself as savior of his family ("I rescued you") and madly decides to go deeper into the jungle. "We cannot go back," he explains. "Why?" asks his wife. "Because [a moment of hesitation] it's not there any

more . . . a cataclysm . . . the end of that world." "That was Jeron-imo!" his wife corrects him. But Allie knows better: "No, I'm telling you about the United States of America."

Theroux's *The Mosquito Coast* is permeated with the myth of Pro-metheus, and Luebke sees this myth as crucial to the novel (Luebke, 230–31). There are, however, only traces of the Promethean myth in Schrader's script, which focuses on the protagonist's downfall with-out providing this broader mythological dimension. Allie Fox tries to bring technology to the jungle natives, tries to save them ("I'm here to help you"), and, like Prometheus, is attacked by vultures at the moment of his death. With Prometheus, he also shares his sense of mission and the responsibility for all of humankind's problems. "I'm the last man!" he states, heading for the Mosquitian district in Hon-duras. Once there he creates an ice-making plant, appropriately named "Fat Boy," which overlooks Jeronimo ("ice is civilization"). He tries to deliver this symbol of civilization to the inland natives; but after days of travel the block of ice has melted and he arrives with water—a symbolic scene that demonstrates the futility of his schemes. The natives at Jeronimo take not only ice for granted but also air conditioning and cold water, which upsets Allie.

For Bruce Bawer, *The Mosquito Coast* also works as an allegory of the bonds between fathers and sons.[6] His comment is true only with regard to the novel, in which the confrontation between the father and his two sons is a key element. Weir's adaptation, which focuses on the protagonist, bypasses this opportunity and tells the story of the unrestrained, mad individualist who endangers his family and himself in pursuit of his utopian visions. Allie's oldest son is a commentator rather than an active participant. As he enters into manhood, the film reflects his disenchantment with (but not open rebellion against) his father. The younger, eleven-year-old Jerry (Jadrien Steele) is more critical. After the destruction of Jeronimo, the boys start to resent their father's tyrannical regime. They are disillusioned with him, but not confrontational.

The Mosquito Coast is framed by two voice-overs from Charlie about his father. Charlie's "I grew up with the belief that the world belonged to him and everything he said was true" is placed at the beginning of the film. After Allie's death, Charlie's voice-over ends the film: "Once I believed in father, and the world had seemed small and old. Now he was gone and I wasn't afraid to love him any more. And the world seemed limitless." This is, however, a postscript more

appropriate to the novel, with its focus on the relationship between father and son, than to the film, with its focus on the steady decline of the protagonist into madness.

On the other hand, Weir's *The Mosquito Coast,* like Theroux's novel, is also about adventure. Many sequences, particularly those showing the beauty of the machines and mechanisms created by Allie Fox, have the charm of a Jules Verne novel; the sequences are full of the praises of human beings, their knowledge and thoughts. "Science is worse than magic," the villagers maintain while helping Allie Fox's dream come true, in a sense foretelling the film's tragic ending.

The Mosquito Coast considers a classic hero to be an inseparable part of the American tradition, a type also present in two of Weir's earlier films. At first glance, Allie Fox appears to be a typical American hero, a strong individual with relentless energy, an embodiment of the American dream. As opposed to the reporter in *The Year of Living Dangerously* (an Australian, but built on an American model), and the honest police detective from *Witness,* Fox is an obsessive character, an egocentric megalomaniac madly pursuing his vision of the world. He is also presented as the embodiment of genius. "My father is a genius," says Charlie. A little later, however, he also perceives the other side of genius: madness.

The Mosquito Coast can thus be seen as yet another story about American individualism, inventiveness, and emulation, about an American dream—but without a typical happy ending. Weir's choice of Harrison Ford for the leading part is not a coincidence. His name personifies the optimistic side of the American parable of unlimited possibilities: the screen characters of Han Solo in George Lucas's *Star Wars* trilogy and Indiana Jones in Steven Spielberg's trio of adventure films. But *The Mosquito Coast* should be taken as the dark story of a strong personality, a film destroying myths of individual omnipotence, a film concerning, as Weir says, "an American tragedy" (McGilligan, 30).

In the opening scenes Allie Fox works as a handyman for an asparagus farmer, Mr. Polski (Dick O'Neill), who calls Allie "the worst kind of pain in the neck, a know-it-all who is sometimes right," and "a dangerous man." Allie's task is to create a simple cooling system for the barn where Polski keeps his asparagus. This task, however, is not challenge enough for a genius of Allie's caliber. Instead, he creates a small machine, a tiny model of the huge ice-making machine he will build in Jeronimo, "Fat Boy." Mr. Polski's rejection of the machine convinces Allie of the necessity to leave the country.

Weir's work deals mostly with the protagonist's weaknesses: the way in which the main character is portrayed indicates that *The Mosquito Coast* can be taken as an ironic comment on the American tradition of a strong leading man. Even if he refuses to believe it, Allie Fox does not have before him a future of unlimited possibilities.

Watching Allie's behavior, the viewer follows Charlie's evolution from enchantment to total disillusionment with his father. The film begins like the novel, with the same dark vision of the United States and Fox's tirades about the decline of America. The protagonist is disenchanted with American civilization, and numerous examples presented in the film support his view, showing an America that is corrupt, flooded with foreign goods and foreign workers, certainly not a place for people like Allie Fox. Though Weir claims that his film was not intended to be a kind of social commentary on America (McGilligan, 32), Schrader's script sounds that way nonetheless. The vision of the United States is dark, quite different from the pastoral, rural America portrayed in *Witness*. "This country is going to the dogs," states Allie. The United States is full of crime and drugs, morally bankrupt, leaving Fox with the single option of saying "have a nice day America" and escaping into the jungle.

In the jungle, however, Fox also feels threatened when he meets another strong personality, Spellgood. Fox and Spellgood are, to a certain extent, similar: both are hungry for new souls and unconquered territories, both demand total loyalty from their families and believers. Their first meeting on the ship to the Mosquito Coast foreshadows the power struggle to come. Fox corrects Spellgood on a point in the Bible and refuses to take a gift: "the latest, the blue-jeans bible," which was "designed by the psychologists." Their next meeting at Jeronimo is a real battle for territory. In a westernlike scene, Spellgood and his two native followers enter Fox's camp. They are pictured in a low-angle shot from behind, a scene reminiscent of the scene from *Witness* in which the corrupt policemen enter the Amish settlement. Framed from behind, Fox, whose work tools look like a holster and gun, meets his enemy. The "duel" is a fierce exchange of verbal accusations. "The Lord hasn't any idea this place exists," says Fox, "or if he did he would have done something for these people a long time ago. But he didn't. I did!" The missionary is thus forced to abandon this territory. Their next meeting is disastrous. While setting Spellgood's church on fire (Fox calls the mission a "Christian concentration camp," on noticing the barbed wire surrounding it), he is shot by the preacher and, as a result, paralyzed.

Fox's "Fat Boy" and Spellgood's mission function as symbols of conquest of the land, of control over "their" territories. The ice-making plant is Fox's "church" of unrestrained technological progress. Heightened by the camera's low-angle shots, "Fat Boy" towers above the region. Its small prototype in Massachusetts is filmed in a corresponding fashion when taken by Fox and his sons to the asparagus farmer. Spellgood's mission is similarly framed by the camera. Eventually, both "churches" go up in flames.

Another threat to the hero is a group of armed bandits, perhaps guerillas, who want to settle in the paradise Fox has built. While visiting an Indian camp, Fox, thinking they are prisoners, tells them how to escape and invites them to Jeronimo. They come and take over Fox's colony. Fox's attempt to rid himself of them marks the beginning of the misfortunes that befall his family and that eventually lead to his madness. Fox tries to freeze the intruders in "Fat Boy," where he has offered them shelter. Their desperate attempt to shoot their way out results in an explosion and their death, the destruction of Jeronimo, and the pollution of the area. Ironically, the explosion of "Fat Boy" and the contamination of Jeronimo with ammonium hydroxide serves as a remainder of the protagonist's early comments on the threat of nuclear annihilation to the United States.

In Weir's interpretation, *The Mosquito Coast* can be taken as a comment on the American spirit as well as a picture of mental illness. On a psychological level, the journey into the jungle is a journey into the self, a journey into the Conradian "heart of darkness." Fox's withdrawal from society ("this place is a toilet") and his megalomania ("I am your salvation" and "I am the last man") mark him for madness. This withdrawal is both psychological (Allie talks but does not listen, demonstrating antisocial behavior) and physical (he leaves the country). In some respects Fox is reminiscent of another Weir character: the lawyer in *The Last Wave*. Each is convinced of his unique role and, in pursuing his goal, gradually descends into madness.

"I am Dr. Frankenstein," Fox says in the novel, after creating his "Fat Boy" ice-making plant (Theroux, 155). In the film, before delivering the small prototype to Mr. Polski, he introduces his invention to his sons as a machine with near-human qualities. During the scene, in the background of Fox's workshop, a picture of a human skeleton hangs. "It is human inside. Its entrails and vitals: that's his digestive system, circulatory system, respiration, lungs, fatty tissues, kidneys, pneuma, . . . his plasma." When asked what it is, he does not

hesitate: "It's perfection," he explains proudly, just as Dr. Frankenstein might have said of his creation.

Fox is a perfectionist who wants to correct God's imperfect creations. In the film's finale he confesses to Charlie: "It's a bad design, the human body. Skin is not thick enough, too little hair, no claws, fangs. We were not meant to stand upright. It exposes our heart and genitals. We should be on our fours."

Fox's desire for perfection ("We are not perfect") is reminiscent of Frankenstein's desire to defy nature. Moreover, like Frankenstein, he, too, is betrayed by his creation. The explosion of "Fat Boy," which produces a minor apocalypse for the Foxes and for Jeronimo's population, is the beginning of the end for Fox. He must abandon the place he has colonized. In his last words, "Nature is crooked. I wanted right angles and straight lines," Fox admits defeat.

The Mosquito Coast differs distinctly from Weir's earlier works. This difference mainly involves the manner in which the main protagonist is treated. Unlike his previous works, and unlike Theroux's novel, this film does not involve the spectator in the protagonist's adventures. The camera persistently follows Fox's nonstop talking and demonstrations of his new inventions. Particularly in the scenes showing the building of Jeronimo, the camera ridicules the protagonist and his jeremiads to the natives on the conditions of life in the United States. These speeches are as comprehensible to the locals as Spellgood's video-recorded jungle preaching, in which he says that saying "a prayer" is "just as simple as making a telephone call" (the locals, of course, have no access to telephones).

In the final part of the film, which takes place on an inhospitable beach of the Atlantic coast, Fox declares that his vision is to live "in harmony with nature." At the same time he scavenges like the vultures he hates.[7] Ironically, we are reminded of his behavior in the United States, where rather than purchasing parts for his inventions he looked for them at the junkyard. Fox, in Weir's interpretation, is a paranoiac and egomaniac, a madman and a narcissist, a man driven by his perception of the American dream. He is a tragicomic hero whose tragedy the viewer cannot take seriously because it is never taken as such by Weir.

Prior to *The Mosquito Coast,* Weir's treatment of protagonists had been serious; the more ordinary they were, the more solemn the attitude toward them, sometimes slightly tinged with irony. *The Mosquito Coast,* a film about an unusual character, is, as Richard Combs correctly remarks, "an unobsessive film about an obsessive character"

Harrison Ford (Allie Fox) with Helen Mirren (as "Mother," Fox's wife), adrift on a jungle river in *The Mosquito Coast* (1986), following the destruction of their utopian community.

(Combs 1987, 53). Even the last, tragic sequences do not beg the viewer's involvement. The director maintains distance from the protagonist, thus depriving *The Mosquito Coast* of the mood of, for example, Werner Herzog's films staged in similar circumstances and with comparable characters played by Klaus Kinsky: *Aguirre, Wrath of God* (1972) and *Fitzcarraldo* (1982).

Herzog's films are also about visionaries driven by the desire to establish their own communities in the jungles of South America. In *Fitzcarraldo* there is the desire to bring opera to the jungle, in *Aguirre, Wrath of God,* to conquer a new land. In both cases the protagonists are obsessed adventurers eager to bring their visions to life at any cost. In Herzog's films, however, the passion (or perhaps creative madness?) is on both sides of the camera: they are obsessive films about obsessive characters.

Certainly, *The Mosquito Coast* cannot be classified as Weir's finest achievement. The director did not attain what seems crucial for his artistic success: a mysterious, oneiric mood. The characters are unconvincing, and the atmosphere is devoid of curiosity. However, in spite of visible stylistic dissimilarities, *The Mosquito Coast* contains patterns similar to Weir's earlier films, among them an interest in cultural clashes, ironic comments on pop culture, carefully composed images, and at least a sense of the mysterious that drives protagonists toward something unknown and potentially dangerous. On the one hand, *The Mosquito Coast* is a further attempt to develop the more concrete, less mysterious narrative strategy Weir began with *Gallipoli.* On the other hand, *The Mosquito Coast* is not imprinted with Weir's characteristic style; his favorite themes are hidden within the narrative line, rendering them weaker and less convincing.

Compared with the painterly images of *Witness,* the photography in *The Mosquito Coast* is more realistic, sometimes even documentary in mood (the portrayal of Massachusetts, the jungle, etc.). John Seale, director of photography and one of Weir's frequent collaborators, does not beautify reality in *The Mosquito Coast;* his frequently moving camera reflects the restless spirit of the protagonist. In Seale's words, the camera is always behind Fox, "trying to keep up, just like his family."[8]

Thus *The Mosquito Coast,* in spite of its similarities to Weir's earlier productions, appears to mark a change in style. The director emphasizes that this evolution was conscious. He was, he says, "looking for ways to force change" on himself, to "remove" himself from the film.

"I am looking for a way to eliminate, to simplify, to rely on fewer tricks and gimmicks, and in a way I've been trying to do that for years" (McGilligan, 32). According to Weir, he filmed *The Mosquito Coast* in very conventional style so as "not to repel the viewer." As further justification for this shift, Weir suggests that the unconventionality of the story, with its exploration of marginal ideology, merited a different kind of filmic treatment (McGilligan, 30).

The auteur critics often admire films that prove themselves to be auteur films. *The Mosquito Coast* is a disappointment not because it differs in content from Weir's earlier films but because in it he gives up his personal style and fails to replace it with something equally interesting.[9] Weir sees his conscious effort to change as a sort of "personal cultural revolution" (McGilligan, 30). From history we have learned that every revolution generates its own victims.

CHAPTER 9

Carpe Diem: Idealism versus Realism in *Dead Poets Society*

People are hungry. *Dead Poets* and films like *My Left Foot* and *Henry V* are showing that people want more rich and thoughtful movies.
> —Peter Weir, interview with Katharine Tulich

To many moviegoers Keating has seemed a true hero. . . . We might simply say that too many people are susceptible to the pied piperism of a charmer who feels undervalued by the system.
> —Robert B. Heilman, "The Great-Teacher Myth"

The intriguingly titled film *Dead Poets Society* (1989) portrays an inspiring, eccentric English teacher, John Keating (Robin Williams), at a New England boys' preparatory boarding school, Welton Academy. The film focuses on the conflict between a group of students who are about to make their first adult choices and the conformist world embodied by their rigid school and oppressive parents. The film traces Keating's relationship with his students and centers on his unorthodox teaching methods as well as the impact they have on the boys' lives.

As in his two previous films, Weir confronts his protagonist, a newcomer from the outside world, with a world of unusual beauty whose norms have long since been established and have always been

strictly obeyed. The closely knit religious community of the Amish in *Witness* and the tropical jungle of Central America in *The Mosquito Coast* are replaced with a school imitating Eton—England's famous preparatory school for boys. Here, too, the newcomer–intruder must ultimately fail when confronted with an environment governed by its own principles.

Dead Poets Society is among Weir's most successful films. Apart from winning international recognition, like the British BAFTA Award for best picture and Italy's Donatello Award for best direction, it also received four Academy Award nominations and one award, for best screenplay by Tom Schulman.

In its narrative, Weir's film is not an innovative work. Rather, it recycles old plots and builds them into a very emotional spectacle. *Dead Poets Society* is one of a numerous group of films dealing with inspiring teachers, from *Goodbye Mr. Chips* (1939) to *Stand and Deliver* (1988). Bruce Bawer accurately points out that Weir's film deals with the same theme as *The Prime of Miss Jean Brodie* (1969), directed by Robert Neame.[1] In both films, the teachers (Miss Brodie and her later counterpart, Keating) can be seen as more interested in self-adulation than in the educational process. Both seem to have a narcissistic need for the students' admiration. *Dead Poets Society* is also related to a group of distinguished, antiestablishment films depicting oppressive school systems, Jean Vigo's *Zéro de conduite* (1933) and Lindsay Anderson's *If . . .* (1968) being the best-known examples. However, while both aforementioned films are borderline surrealist satires, *Dead Poets Society* is a serious, lyrical, and romantically idealistic work. The theme of the hardship of puberty, magnified by the oppressiveness of the boarding school, also appears in some renowned Australian New Wave films, such as Fred Schepisi's *The Devil's Playground* (1976) and Bruce Beresford's *The Getting of Wisdom* (1977), not to mention Weir's *Picnic at Hanging Rock*.

From the opening credits, *Dead Poets Society* introduces a mood resembling that of *Picnic at Hanging Rock*. It is fall 1959, the beginning of another year at Welton Academy, a secluded and exclusive boys' school set in the colorful, tranquil hills of Vermont. The grandiose opening ceremony includes bagpipe music, candles carried by each student, and a pompous introductory speech by the headmaster. The school's principles—"tradition, honor, discipline, excellence" (the student version of which is "travesty, horror, decadence and excrement")—are displayed on banners and recited at the inauguration of the new academic year. Intensified by Maurice Jarre's

Robin Williams (standing) as the charismatic English professor John Keating "performing" for his class. From *Dead Poets Society* (1989).

sublime musical score, John Seale's camera captures the boys' thrilled faces and the nervous atmosphere of excitement. In a similarly inspired atmosphere, Mrs. Appleyard's schoolgirls start their journey toward Hanging Rock. Two of them never return.

Dead Poets Society does indeed share many similarities with *Picnic at Hanging Rock:* the primordial Hanging Rock is replaced by the equally mystical Indian cave—both of which have sexual meaning— and schoolgirls are replaced with schoolboys. A traditional, oppressive school run by a sinister headmaster is common to both films. Mr. Nolan (Norman Lloyd) performs a role similar to that of Mrs. Appleyard in *Picnic at Hanging Rock*. Furthermore, like Appleyard College, Welton Academy is an isolated, solid set of buildings overlooking a picturesque landscape. In both films, there is also a conflict between the closed and ordered world of traditional values, represented by the austere schools, and the resourcefulness and spirit of youth.

Nonetheless, *Dead Poets Society* is not merely a male version of *Picnic at Hanging Rock*. The title of the film comes from the name of a group founded by Keating when he was himself a student at Welton. The group members were dedicated to "sucking the marrow out of life," as Keating explains to his pupils. Now seven of his students secretly revive the society by holding nighttime gatherings in a nearby cave: they read poetry, play the saxophone, and socialize. This

outwardly innocent act, however, is perceived as an act of defiance by the school authorities.

Dead Poets Society continues Weir's classic poetics of contrast and is built around opposing themes and ideas:

> School versus cave
> Knowledge versus imagination
> Adults versus youths
> Realism versus idealism
> Rationalism versus romanticism
> Conformity versus personal freedom

Visually, Weir contrasts Welton's pseudo-Gothic buildings with the primitiveness of the cave, youthful exuberance with the oppressive system of education, realistic conventions of the day with the freedom of the night. All contribute to the primary theme of the film— the choice that must be made between the pursuit of personal freedom and expression and a life of safe conformity.

On the surface, this is another film about the effect of a charismatic teacher on a group of students. What is hidden beneath the surface of the story, however, is the idealistic, typically Weirian view that nature is always repressed by culture. As usual, Weir sides with nature, and in doing so, presents a clear distinction between the spirited world of personal freedom (Keating and his followers) and the strict world of oppressive pragmatism (the rest of the teachers and the parents). The situation in the film is black and white; there's no opportunity for compromise. Everything is geared toward Keating's being made a scapegoat of the establishment while simultaneously realizing a moral victory.

In its presentation of characters, the film is transparent and manipulates the viewer's emotions to achieve an easy final effect. Weir separates the good from the bad. *Dead Poets Society* portrays a one-dimensional fictional world with a clear division between progressive and conservative, young and old. Weir's Welton Academy is a model of the rigid educational institution; his charismatic protagonist is the quintessence of what an inspiring teacher ought to be. Keating's students serve only as the inert objects of his manipulation. His style of teaching is contrasted with that of other teachers: passionate and inspired as opposed to routine and boring; their methods fail to elicit any emotional response from the students.

As presented in the film, the world of adults and authority figures is utterly bad; Keating is the exception to the rule. Parents in *Dead Poets Society* consist of caricatures of tyrannical bourgeois fathers, obedient wives and voiceless mothers. In a sense, the title of the film inadvertently refers to their (adult) world. This is a generation of dead poets who have lost their sensitivity, their sense of freedom, not to mention their idealistic, youthful aspirations. The film seems to suggest that in growing older one has to kill an inner poet; the choice has to be made between seizing the day and undertaking a disciplined (in the film's context: boring) life. As usual, Weir sides with youth, imagination, and rebellion.

"Carpe diem," says Keating during the inaugural lesson. Seize the day. "Make your lives extraordinary!" He encourages his students to learn to think for themselves and to find their own voice. The film is safely set in the late 1950s, when conservative norms flourished relatively unchallenged. Keating's statements are harbingers of the rebellious 1960s, revolutionary in a school whose main task is to cultivate the future political and business elite of the United States. Theater and poetry are understood only as ornaments to the "more useful" subjects. The boys' future has been carefully planned by their parents, who will steer them to Ivy League universities and, eventually, to successful professional careers.

In Robin Williams's memorable interpretation, Keating, though he belongs to the realm of adult wisdom (but also boredom and routine), also represents the world of youthful rebellion and imagination. Like the majority of Weir's earlier protagonists (from Michael to John Book), Keating acts as a mediator between these two different worlds. He attempts to bring together what is incompatible: anarchy and order, youth and experience, day and night. How a man like Keating finds himself at Welton in 1959 remains the screenwriter's (Tom Schulman's) unsolved mystery.

The Keating persona has provoked many negative critical responses. For Robert B. Heilman, Keating, who is "a hot on-stage performer," belongs to the "Great Teacher" category, whose representatives are remembered not for their teaching but for their theatrics. The opposite, "the good teacher," cares about knowledge and is focused on his students.[2] According to Bawer, Keating is portrayed as "a lonely, self-romanticizing egoist whose classroom style fosters a personality cult" (Bawer, 40). The critic also asserts that the film is unforgivably callow and sentimental about its subject: it promotes its hero, who, instead of teaching, adores boys "like a neurotically posses-

sive mother" (Bawer, 49). To attract their attention, for instance, Keating mimics different famous actors reciting Shakespeare. The emphasis is on histrionics not on education. The strongest attack, however, comes from John Simon, for whom this is "the most dishonest movie, . . . a particularly plummy specimen of the pseudo-sensitive, pseudo-serious, pseudo-real film."[3]

Pamela A. Rooks argues that *Dead Poets Society*, instead of questioning values represented by the Welton Academy, rather reinforces them "in an unfortunate triumph of style over substance."[4] Harry M. Geduld seems to share her point of view. He believes that Keating wants his students not to make their own choices but to copy him, and in this he is successful. Geduld points out that "Keating is a con-artist, not a brilliant teacher, and his students are his misguided victims. He performs stunts that underscore his persona instead of teaching literature."[5] In the powerful, emotional climax, in which students, in a gesture of respect for Keating, climb on their desktops in order, as Keating puts it, to "see the world from a different angle," they are, according to Geduld, only imitating one of Keating's "stunts." Rooks makes a similar point: "The dynamics of the scene are such that not to stand on the desk would have been the true expression of individualism" (Rooks, 77).

Given the film's potential, Weir's work disappoints; it is a conventional film about an unconventional character. Like Keating's style of teaching, Weir's film prefers easy effects over substance. *Dead Poets Society* targets the viewers' emotions, which during the first viewing overpower any attempt at reasoning. For instance, in an emotional and well-executed scene, Keating wants his students to rip out the preface, a scholarly, passionless tract, from their *Understanding Poetry* textbooks. Poetry cannot be measured, says Keating, cannot be described in quantitative terms. He does not, however, offer any real counterproposition: "feeling" and "passion" are his only choices. In the last sequence of the film, the headmaster, Keating's replacement for the English class, returns to the realist writers Keating had omitted from the curriculum: the final triumph of realism over romanticism.

Unlike most of Weir's films, *Dead Poets Society* is not about the effects of occurrences beyond the protagonist's control but about the impact of an individual on a small group of people. The English teacher, when a student at Welton himself, had been voted "The Man Most Likely to Do Anything." On one hand, Keating wants to encourage

the boys' initiative; he wants them to respond to the beauty of language and express themselves in a unique way. On the other hand, he manipulates his students, the effects of which contribute to the death of one, Neil Perry (Robert Sean Leonard).

The theme of death permeates the film right from its uplifting beginning and, in a sense, foreshadows Neil's suicide. For critic John Carroll, Keating, though he brings a liberating spirit to the school, functions also as an "emissary of death."[6] In an introductory scene the teacher shows a photograph taken in 1902 that pictures former Welton students, now all presumably dead. When he remarks that "these boys are now fertilizing daffodils," the camera captures Neil's uneasy smile. "We are food for worms, lads!" states Keating, who then offers the alternative: carpe diem, seize the day, do not waste your life, make it extraordinary. In a later scene, Keating invokes Walt Whitman's "O Captain, My Captain," a poem referring to Abraham Lincoln's death. In another scene, during the Poets Society meeting in the cave, Neil reads a passage from Henry David Thoreau's *Walden:* "I went to the woods because I wished to live deliberately, to front only the essential facts of life, and see if I could not learn what it had to teach, and not, when I came to die, discover that I had not lived."

Neil's suicide does not function in the film as an act of rebellion. The struggle between Neil and his domineering father (Kurtwood Smith), which constitutes the most important subplot of the film, can only be, according to the film's philosophy, resolved in one way. Neil, a gifted, all-A student, defies his father's orders ("You will go to Harvard and you will be a doctor") to pursue his artistic goals: he wants to become an actor. In spite of his father's objections, he plays the figure of Puck in a school production of *A Midsummer Night's Dream.* Unable either to convince his father to see things his way or to obey his father's orders, Neil chooses death. The cost of pursuing one's dream is high in this movie: for Charlie Dalton (Gale Hansen) it is expulsion from school; for Neil, death. The suicide is the only romantic solution to Neil's problems: trapped between his personal desires and parental demands, he shoots himself with his father's gun. The suicide scene invokes some painfully obvious symbolic, religious connotations: half-naked Neil slowly takes off Puck's crown, which resembles a Christ-like crown of thorns, and silently stands in front of an open window. Maurice Jarre's music introduces a sombre mood. In a slow-motion scene, he goes downstairs to get his father's gun. The suicide itself is seen only through his father's reaction to it. He suddenly wakes up and, visibly disturbed, gets out of bed. He dis-

covers his son's body and, in an extreme slow-motion shot, rushes toward him. The viewer is not able to see Neil's body. Like the girls in *Picnic at Hanging Rock,* he has moved into a different realm.

Visually, *Dead Poets Society* belongs to the most arresting of Weir's films. It is enhanced by the masterful photography of John Seale, who worked with Weir as a camera operator as early as in the production of *Picnic at Hanging Rock.* Seale's camera catches images of Welton's countryside bathed first in gold and green and later in snow: autumnal images are followed by snowy winter landscapes. Stanley Kauffmann emphasizes that Seale "shoots the seasons of the year like archetypal statements."[7] The photography creates the film's dramatic mood; as in *Witness,* the story is told through images and every image strengthens the story. In this sense, *Dead Poets Society* is one of Weir's most controlled works. The director avoids a surplus of dialogue and achieves the emotional impact purely cinematographically, through the precisely composed mise-en-scène. Williams and the group of young actors are in a way submitted by the camera. Faces in close-up, which create intimacy, dominate the frame. The young actors do not act but simply *are* in the film, totally subjugated to the camera.

The atmosphere of *Dead Poets Society* is achieved by mise-en-scène, camera movement, and music (Maurice Jarre's fourth collaboration with Weir). In one of the film's most spectacular scenes, the director portrays the students going to their first nightly meeting in the cave. Wearing hooded jackets, the boys run in slow motion from the dormitory through woods toward the cave. A fog and a surreal blue light accompany the scene and enhance the atmosphere of mystery. The meeting resembles a secret fantastic ceremony. All gatherings in the cave are shot with unusual lighting of the boys' faces: each student holds a flashlight, then, during later meetings, a fire in the cave provides a source of light. Music in *Dead Poets Society* serves to enhance intimacy and the romantic spirit. Fond of classical music, Weir utilizes Beethoven's Symphony No. 9 in the soccer match scene, which, shown partly in slow motion, stresses the students' physical liberation, which, presumably, will later result in their spirits being freed as well. Jarre's familiar tones are reminiscent of the atmosphere in *Witness* and perform a similar role; the combination of imagery and sublime music creates the films' distinct narrative rhythm.

In a gesture similar to that used in his biggest Australian success, *Picnic at Hanging Rock,* Weir supports the story with glimpses of

nature. Images of the landscape and wildlife surrounding Welton are intertwined with the boys' activities: in the morning during the first day of classes, the shot of flocks of wild ducks clumsily rising to flight is intercut with the beginning of school. In another scene, when Knox Overstreet (Josh Charles) rides his bicycle to see Chris, a stereotypical blond woman he is in love with, the birds start to fly upward symbolizing Knox's animated mind ("Carpe diem, even if it kills me!").

In contrast with *The Mosquito Coast*, the director retains precise control of mood and atmosphere. *Dead Poets Society* is, however, perceived by some critics as "overprepared"[8] and "intensely old fashioned."[9] Pauline Kael, who is often critical of Weir's films, notes in her review that this is "conservative craftsmanship. . . . The picture draws out the obvious and turns itself into a classic." According to Kael, like *Gallipoli*, *Dead Poets Society* is a prestige picture, "with a gold ribbon attached to it" (Kael 1989, 71). In another, often-quoted text she makes a similar claim on Australian cinema as a whole. She emphasizes the lack of excitement in Antipodean cinema and remarks that watching Australian films from the 1970s is "like reading an old-fashioned novel. . . . There is a security in a certain kind of film for an audience and 'Made in Australia' is almost like a seal of Good Housekeeping in a film.[10]

Kael sees classic (AFC) Australian films as worthy but dull, and she refers to the British classic film *Chariots of Fire* (1981) as "the best Australian film made outside Australia" (Kael 1988, 68). Her comments on the conservative nature of Australian films can be extended to *Dead Poets Society*, a film that, ironically, attempts to attack conservatism and to promote an antiestablishment viewpoint. In spite of this, the film is of a safe nature, superficially refined in presenting its conflict, and belongs in the familiar domain of high-quality television productions.[11]

The Year of Living Dangerously already represented a partial exercise in melodrama. Neither in *Dead Poets Society* does Weir avoid some elements of melodrama; the final frames of the film are among the most emotionally powerful in contemporary cinema. Nevertheless, Schulman's script is sometimes too close to television soap opera. Most of the subplots seem to be taken from the familiar realm of television (for instance, Knox Overstreet's love for his cheerleader, Chris Noel, and Todd Anderson's [Ethan Hawke] struggle to overcome exceptional shyness and find his own voice). Last but not least,

the conflict between the dogmatic father and the son, an aspiring actor, resembles the stock conflict of a prime-time television production. Weir strengthens these familiar images and creates an equilibrium between "art film" and "TV movie."

The evolution of Todd Anderson constitutes the most absorbing subplot in *Dead Poets Society*. A disturbingly inarticulate character in the first part of the film, who is often contrasted with his brilliant older brother, tries to define himself. Keating comments that Todd "thinks everything inside him is worthless and embarrassing." The well-known line from Whitman's "Song of Myself"—"I sound my barbaric yawp over the rooftops of the world"—is used by the teacher to persuade his pupil to speak. Finally, he is "cured" by Keating, who encourages him to simply be himself; to speak in his unique voice without fear ("yell like a man!"). In the final frames of the film, it is Todd who initiates "rebellion" after the suicide of his roommate, Neil, and the dismissal of Keating.[12]

Weir makes a traditional film with a 1960s flavor. *Dead Poets Society* is not a fighting film but rather an overtly sentimental work that sacrifices its narrative potential for romantic, clichéd imagery. Its ideology

Robin Williams (John Keating) trying to help his student, Ethan Hawke (Todd Anderson), overcome his painful shyness. From *Dead Poets Society* (1989).

of individualism, its call for "finding one's own way" and rebellion are portrayed in a safe romantic way. The social reality in the film is sketchy and sacrificed for transparent symbolic gesture. Weir prefers the elevated and the romantic over the uneasiness and turbulence of teenagehood. The finale of the film, when the boys stand on their desks to follow one of Keating's examples, is the only logical end to the film. There is no real rebellion in the film—everything is lost in the lyrical, lofty romantic mist.

Dead Poets Society continues a mode Weir took up in *Witness*. The preoccupation with imagery, with details, is accompanied by the faultless control over the atmosphere of the film and the precise arrangement of dramatic moments. As a rule, Weir pays great attention to details, which he chooses effectively and, I suspect, intuitively. To the qualities already well known from his Australian period, Weir adds a competence for building and relieving tension and an inner discipline, which is, to a certain extent, imposed by Hollywood screenplays. Still, in spite of a more mainstream orientation, the director is able to preserve his personal style and to deal with issues that have long occupied him.

CHAPTER 10

A Parisian in America: *Green Card*

Green Card is a test case, actually. It's an *auteur* film, made overseas by an Australian director, with the involvement of French components.

—Peter Weir, interview with Katharine Tulich

Green is a color of hope. A green card (which in fact is no longer green), means hope for many immigrants. Peter Weir's *Green Card* (1993) deals with a green card marriage that turns into real love, crossing barriers of culture and language. An Australian-French coproduction set in New York, *Green Card* is Weir's most controlled work to date: he acts as writer, director, and, for the first time, producer. The screenplay, as the director admits, was written specifically for Gérard Depardieu and to a certain degree draws on the biography of the French star.[1]

Green Card is a sentimental comedy of manners reminiscent of the romantic, screwball comedies of the 1940s and 1950s. It is also, as Verina Glaessner remarks, an "escapist fairy-tale" with a "sub-Roegian metaphysic."[2] We can accept without question the first part of Glaessner's comment: the film offers an escapist narrative, though without a definite happy ending. The "sub-Roegian metaphysic," however, by which we may understand a realm of enigma, present in Weir's earlier works, is missing. Instead, *Green Card* is a transparent comedy of manners that sustains Weirian auteurist touches. The film's humor relies principally on the juxtaposition of two presumably

incompatible ways of life and two supposedly incompatible persons whose differences are conquered by love.

The film's protagonist, the enigmatic Frenchman Georges Fauré (Depardieu), wants to get a working visa, a green card, so he can get a job in the United States. (We will leave aside the ridiculous question as to why a French subject would be so desperate to work in the New World.) The only way he sees to accomplish this is to marry an American citizen. Brontë Parrish (Andie MacDowell), a native of New York, is also interested in a marriage of convenience but for a completely different reason: she wants to get a Manhattan apartment with a magnificent greenhouse, which is available only to married couples. Though Brontë and Georges do not know each other, their common friend, Anton, arranges a paper marriage to solve their "existential problems." Brontë does not even think of informing her parents or her boyfriend, Phil (Gregg Edelman), of her unorthodox decision. Her "husband," Georges, is not even able to learn her proper name (he calls her Betty instead of Brontë). Initially Brontë and Georges get what they want. But their marriage of convenience ("You don't have to see him again") turns into a marriage of inconvenience with the appearance of government investigators.

The inquiry of an immigration authority functions as the outside force beyond visible control that is common to Weir's films. It brings Brontë and Georges together, forcing them to share Brontë's flat for a weekend and learn about each other so they will be able to convince the authorities that theirs is a bona fide marriage. The opposites that originally repelled begin to attract.

In spite of the straightforward narrative and intended lack of sophistication, *Green Card* is in line with Weir's other films. As in his other works, the film's energy comes from the clash of characters representing two different cultures. Contrary to most of Weir's earlier films, the mutual discoveries in *Green Card* lead the protagonists to romance and a possibly solid future relationship. Their emotional separation at the end of the film brings sorrow as well as hope of future reunion.

The prime source of comedy in *Green Card* is the apparent irreconcilability of the leading characters. Their initial meeting at Café Afrika clearly demonstrates this: Brontë first sees Georges from behind the window and a look of uneasiness, perhaps disappointment, appears on her face. He is introduced as a composer ("Are you related to the Faurées?"—he is asked later at the Adlers' dinner

party), though his behavior and appearance place him in the working class. But he is French. The Frenchness of Georges, his Gallic charm, and his linkage with old European culture are juxtaposed with the snobbish "progressiveness" of Brontë and her New York friends.

Georges is the diametric negation of Brontë: a heavy smoker and drinker, a person who grabs as much as he can from every day of life, an individual with a tough, complex past. Geoffrey Simpson's camera juxtaposes the fleshiness of Depardieu's face, his massive body, and unclean, long hair with Brontë's aseptic, politically correct looks and behavior. Among clean-cut Americans, Georges looks like a visitor from another planet. A porter at Brontë's house, Oscar, who believes Georges's fantastic stories of adventures in Africa, says of Georges's sudden appearance: "When I've first seen you, I thought: this guy just stepped out of the jungle."

Brontë is a member of the Green Guerillas, an inner-city organization dedicated to the greening of the poor neighborhoods of New York. The environment is her prime concern. "You care more for plants than people," remarks an outraged Georges. A middle-class

The very down-to-earth Frenchman Gérard Depardieu (Georges Fauré) with the very uptight New Yorker Andie MacDowell (seated, right, as Brontë Parrish) and Brontë's best friend, played by Bebe Neuwirth. From *Green Card* (1990).

horticulturist and a vegetarian, Brontë is involved with another polit-
ically correct character: the earnest but boring environmentalist, Phil.
"I didn't like Phil," comments Brontë's best friend Lauren Adler
(Bebe Neuwirth), "so earnest, my god." According to the film's logic,
Phil has no chance when competing against the earthy and ebullient
Frenchman.

Brontë is the clichéd incarnation of sterile progressiveness, while
Georges represents what life is all about. He is so full of joie de vivre
that he is nearly unreal, a caricature of Frenchness. "I just wanted to
continue my life as it was before," Brontë declares. "I'm waiting for
my life to begin," states Georges. It is she, however, who may change
under Georges's influence and "go French." Before meeting Georges,
she seems to have no room for personal development ("you live out
of a book," says Georges). She accepts Georges's continental charm
and, in spite of her earlier reservations ("you silly French oaf," "you
are so right-wing about everything," "your manners are atrocious"),
she begins to accept his unhealthy, "decadent" lifestyle. The clash of
the stereotyped French and American ways of life—high fat versus

Brontë and Georges (Andie MacDowell and Gerard Depardieu) make an
effort to document their supposed married life for immigration officials.
From *Green Card* (1990).

skim—structures the film. The viewer laughs not at Georges's habits but at their incompatibility with the world around him.

In the film's opening scene, a young black musician performs in the New York subway. A driving beat on a plastic can introduces a mood resembling that of *The Plumber,* Weir's early film about a similar encounter between a couple from different cultures. In that film, the sound of primitive drums is associated with the uncouth working-class protagonist who invades the privacy of a female would-be academic. This encounter results in a sexual power game, psychological threat, and the final victory of the woman.

Green Card, nonetheless, never moves into this Pinteresque realm. Instead, it rapidly progresses into the domain of operetta. Initial problems, the result of two different backgrounds, are gradually overcome. Everything is geared toward the final victory of love.

The film can be viewed as another variation on the beauty and the beast myth. In *Green Card,* however, the beast remains beast and never thinks about turning into a more acceptable creature. For this is a sophisticated French beast with a Dionysian attitude toward life. There is no question of him turning vegetarian and bodybuilder. Like Dracula and Nosferatu, he "invades" the new world. The anemic beauty, overpowered by the intruder's hypnotic power, can only offer herself. The beauty accepts the beast as a beast; she is defeated by his inner beauty and sophistication.

Comedy is a new genre for Weir, though there are comedic touches in some of his earlier films. Nonetheless, particularly in his "Gothic" period, it is an offbeat sense of humor: bizarre, grotesque, reminiscent of black comedy. *Witness* and *Dead Poets Society* provide comic relief of a different kind: the contrast between the rural and the urban and Robin Williams's "great teacher" show are the sources of comedy. In *Green Card,* Weir pokes fun at the "progressive" concerns of Brontë and her New York friends and at the indulgent, "decadent" behavior of Georges. Only when one is compared with the other does their behavior become a laughing matter. The comedy flourishes particularly in episodes involving brief appearances from Jessie Keosian (whose role could have been better developed) in the character of old Mrs. Bird.

As a rule, Weir does not go too far with his criticism. He provides safe, old-fashioned, teatime laughter, not mockery. The director is

more interested in the melodramatic and the romantic than in comedy per se. His tendency toward sentimentalization prevents the film from going deeper in its account of events. Instead, Weir glides on the surface of phenomena and accommodates clichés. Apart from the characters, for instance, in the scene showing a renovation of a poor inner-city neighborhood, which bears a strong resemblance to *Witness*'s barn-raising scene, Weir approaches cliché in his Disney-like portrayal of communal activities.

Melodrama dominates the film from its opening. The viewer awaits the inevitable final reunion, and his patience is promptly rewarded. In the last scene the action returns to where it began: to the Café Afrika. Through Brontë's eyes the viewer watches the same medium shot of Georges standing behind the window of the coffee shop. Romantic music anticipates the development of the action. Close-ups of long duration of the protagonists' faces are carefully intercut. The final run and embrace follows necessarily. The declaration of love is inevitable. Suddenly, she no longer cares about her greenhouse. In return, he invites her to France. An immigration officer, Mr. Gorski (Ethan Phillips), who escorts Georges to the airport, cannot hide his amazement. The opposites converge in an emotional spectacle applauded by the viewer.

Music greatly contributes to the atmosphere of *Green Card*. Weir's use of music, nevertheless, is not innovative. Rather, he employs familiar scores in familiar situations: classical music for uplifting scenes, sweet pop music for intimacy. Thus Brontë's activities in the conservatory are accompanied by classical music. When she enters her magnificent greenhouse for the first time, Mozart's Flute Concerto No. 1 in G Major conveys her animated state of mind. The dash for the appointment with the immigration authorities is propelled along by Enya's music. The joyful scene in which Brontë and Georges prepare a photographic portfolio for an immigration interview is accompanied by equally cheerful Beach Boys music. (This cliché from myriad mainstream films is unmercifully debunked in numerous comedies, including *Naked Gun* and its sequels.)

The music reinforces the tension between the characters and reveals their state of mind. A dinner party sequence at the Adlers' includes the most braggadocio scene: Georges's impromptu piano solo, which helps Brontë to convince the wealthy hosts to donate their trees to the Green Guerillas. Invited to the party by the Adlers' daughter and Brontë's best friend, Lauren, and introduced as a French

composer, Georges is instantly asked to perform. After producing pure cacophony, which shakes the viewer's belief that he is, in fact, a composer, he moves into the second part of his recital, an emotional appeal to the Adlers. Georges's act reduces the tension between him and Brontë and wins her over.

In another scene, which takes place after the unsuccessful interview with immigration, the lack of music stresses Brontë's emptiness and the sense of loss she feels for her barely initiated love. After the hearing, she is accompanied exclusively by the noises of the street on her way home. Then, when she sits in the conservatory, the only sound is created by a rainfall. This "unnatural" silence stops when Brontë receives Georges's letter, including the score of the melody he used to mumble all the time. The tune fills the soundtrack.

In spite of its thematic affinities with Weir's other films, *Green Card* lacks their sense of mystery. It is an exercise in formula filmmaking. If, in the case of *Witness,* the formula constraints do not prevent Weir from filling the screen with "his" images, the straightforward and cohesive narrative of *Green Card* is paralleled by an equally straightforward film style reminiscent of prime-time television productions. An unconventional love story is conventionally narrated and visualized. The film is transparent and predictable, leaving no room for enigma.

CHAPTER 11

The Days After: *Fearless*

In terms of imagery and rhythm, *Fearless* is a stunning piece of filmmaking. Weir is a far more powerful visual shaman than he was in the days of *The Last Wave*.

—Terrence Rafferty, "After the Crash"

In the nightmarish opening scene of *Fearless,* shot partly in slow motion, a party of people meanders through a cornfield, following Max Klein (Jeff Bridges), who guides them to safety. Carrying an infant, Max appears at the site of a plane crash. Pieces of debris from the plane are scattered across a field. From the air, the crash site looks bizarre; it appears more surreal than tragic. Unsettling sounds strengthen these images of unnatural disaster.

Max wanders through the site with the baby in his arms. The camera creates a sense of devastating disarray by portraying burning parts of the plane, people looking on in horror, passengers' belongings scattered about. After leaving a young boy with some rescuers, Max is directed to a woman crying for her lost child. He leaves the baby with its mother and flees the scene unnoticed. In a hotel room, still in visible shock, he takes a shower and carefully examines his body. He then rents a car and escapes to Los Angeles, without attempting to notify his family. He drives through a desolate desert landscape: his car looks like a lizard crossing the bush in *Picnic at Hanging Rock.* Weir shows Max's amazement at being alive and his loneliness at the same time. Lively music from the Gipsy Kings cuts through the thus-

Jeff Bridges as architect Max Klein, whose remarkable survival of a plane crash for a time rescinds his fear of death. Here he tempts fate by skirting the edge of skyscraper. From *Fearless* (1993).

far muted soundtrack, stressing the affirmation of life, the protagonist's recognition that he is alive.

This mesmerizing Weirian sequence constitutes the opening of *Fearless* (1993), based on a book by Rafael Yglesias, who also authored the script.[1] As in his Australian films, Weir creates a sense of the extraordinary from real occurrences. He portrays an apocalyptic vision similar in spirit to that depicted in *The Last Wave*. Sounds in the opening sequence of *Fearless* resemble in tone the Aboriginal instruments in *The Last Wave* and the eerie, magnified sounds of nature in *Picnic at Hanging Rock*. Though shot in an almost documentary manner, resembling a television report, the opening scene of *Fearless* focuses on the surreal rather than the bodily and the violent. Thus, instead of visceral horror, Weir portrays the plane crash as an event that disrupts natural order, as a violation of nature. Given this, the plane crash in *Fearless* performs the same role as natural elements in Weir's Australian films: it reveals the fragility of human existence and prompts actions that would be impossible under normal circumstances. As in *Picnic at Hanging Rock,* however, Weir focuses on the changes that an uncontrollable occurrence brings to the protagonists' lives rather than on the event itself.

Fearless is not the only film in recent years to deal with a plane crash: *Hero* (1992), directed by Stephen Frears, and *Alive* (1992), directed by Frank Marshall, explore similar territory. Weir, however, is not primarily interested in mocking the media and its celebration of heroism (*Hero*) or in telling an uplifting story about survival in an extreme situation (*Alive*). Weir focuses on the protagonist's reactions in the days after the crash. Like *Alive,* however, *Fearless* attempts to show the plane crash in all its horrifying reality and, in this respect, it supersedes its predecessor.

Certainly, Weir's ability to create a convincingly eerie vision of the crash enhanced the film's critical reception. With the exception of a hostile comment from critic John Simon,[2] *Fearless* was well received. Several critics listed this film as one of the best of 1993.[3]

The plane crash in *Fearless* brings together two people who in ordinary circumstances would have had little chance of meeting. Dr. Bill Perlman (John Turturro), an airline therapist who specializes in post-traumatic stress disorder, hopes to return Max to normality by introducing him to another suffering survivor, Carla Rodrigo (Rosie Perez), a young Puerto Rican woman who lost her child in the crash. Max and Carla share the same experience and the same mys-

tery. Their brush with mortality is more important than their cultural and social differences. "We are safe because we died already," Max later explains to Carla.

Carla is also introduced in the opening sequence. Rescued from the wreckage, she cries for her baby. The plane bursts into flames behind her. She wants to return for her lost child but is forcefully held by rescuers. Then, to the viewer's surprise, it is not she who gets the baby that Max carries but another agonized woman.

After the crash, Carla is withdrawn and depressed. Unlike restless Max, she moves only between her bedroom, full of burning candles and Catholic artifacts, and the neighboring church. She blames herself for the death of her young son, Bubble. During the plane's descent, she held him on her lap, but when the plane crashed she was unable to hold onto him. She is haunted by the idea that she could have prevented her son's death. Like Max, Carla also withdraws from family life and emotionally parts with her husband, Manny (Benicio del Toro), who seems to be more interested in insurance money than in Carla's mental state.

As usual, Weir portrays characters coming from different cultural and social spheres. Max and Carla belong to different social and ethnic strata, but their common experience of death brings them together. Allen Daviau's photography[4] puts the differences between Max and Carla into focus filming their apartments: the comfortable, modern white-washed look of Max's home is juxtaposed with the bright colors of Carla's overcrowded apartment in a Latin American neighborhood. When Max enters her bedroom, the viewer is presented with a different world: candle lights, bright colors, religious artifacts, photographs of her son. Max's WASPish manner is contrasted with Carla's ethnicity and accent; his upper-middle-class world with her working-class world; his lack of religious faith with her religious environment.

In spite of these visible differences, Max and Carla need each other to overcome their problems. After the crash both question the value of their lives. Neither can return to the social roles they successfully performed before. Max perceives himself as the savior of the devastated woman; he brings her back to life. He feels "an overwhelming love" for Carla, as he bluntly confesses to his wife. Furthermore, Max also wants to persuade Carla to "disappear" with him, but fails. Reluctantly rejected by Carla, he undergoes a metamorphosis that ends in his final acceptance of his upper-middle-class, middle-age fate.

As in Weir's earlier films, the characters in *Fearless* are deprived of sexuality. Though sensual tension is created between Carla and Max, it is not acted on.

When compared with Weir's earlier works, the clash of cultures in *Fearless* seems not to be of vital importance. Instead, internal conflict and personality crisis dominate the external political and social predicaments of the film. The characters are drawn together not so much because they differ but because they are united in their brush with death and sense of alienation from their loving but bewildered families. *Fearless,* however, lacks a proper focus and in this respect resembles *The Mosquito Coast* and Weir's futile attempts to make Allie Fox a believable figure. The question of whether *Fearless* is a film about a plane crash, a personality crisis, unfulfilled love, or family melodrama is never answered.

In Yglesias's book, Max is presented in a more ambiguous, almost ironic way. Weir, however, performs the same stratagem as he did in the context of Lindsay's *Picnic at Hanging Rock:* he embraces the solemn and the mysterious at the expense of the ironic. He moves from the rational to the mystical. Whereas the book has two protagonists, Carla and Max, the film almost exclusively presents Max's perspective, to the point of turning, as Terrence Rafferty states, "his character into a Holy Fool."[5]

As we learn about the crash in a series of flashbacks, Max seemingly overcomes his phobia of flying and lapses into unearthly tranquillity. "I'm not afraid. I have no fear," he states while in the plane, immediately after learning the flight is in danger. In slow motion, Max rises from his seat and moves toward a young boy, Byron, who is sitting alone. Among the horrified passengers and crew members, Max appears to be someone with virtually superhuman qualities. The extreme situation requires an extreme response from Max. Facing the inescapable prospect of death, he helps other passengers, comforts them after the plane hits the ground, and, afterward, leads some of the survivors to safety.

After surviving the disaster, Max, a successful San Francisco architect whose routine business flight has been violently disrupted, still seems to be living in the realm of fearlessness he felt during the crash. He seems to be emotionally devastated by the crash and his actions are odd. He tries to live completely without fear and perhaps, according to the film's logic, he even feels immortal. His previous phobia of flying Max shifts into a state of euphoria at being alive. After a near-death experience, he does not hesitate to put his life into jeopardy again and again. He plays with fear and tests his limits: he balances on the edge of the roof of a high-rise building, dashes across a busy San Francisco street, and eats strawberries, to which he has always been deathly (literally) allergic. "I'm past all that," he

explains to a former girlfriend, whom he has not seen for almost twenty years. He also claims that the plane disaster was the best thing that ever happened to him.

Max withdraws from everyday life and alienates his wife, Laura (Isabella Rossellini), as well as an eleven-year-old son, Jonah (Spencer Vrooman). When Laura asks why he disappeared after the crash and neglected to contact her, Max confesses, "I was visiting my past." "Why didn't you tell me?" asks Laura, to which he responds: "I thought I was dead." Max's euphoria prevents him from returning to earth. He cannot, or does not want to, come back to "life." This leads inevitably to marital conflict.

Weir re-creates the crash in a series of six flashbacks scattered throughout the story: four of them are seen from Max's perspective, two from Carla's. He places the entire graphic crash sequence in a powerful flashback scene at the end of the film. In the film's climax, Max almost dies for the second time after eating strawberries—his allergic reaction has returned. His wife and his lawyer desperately try to revive him. As he gasps for breath, he has a vision of the last des-

Jeff Bridges (Max Klein) and Isabella Rossellini (his wife, Laura), a loving couple whose relationship is traumatized by Max's brush with death. From *Fearless* (1993).

perate moments before the crash from the perspective of passengers descending to earth in an out-of-control plane. Intensified by the music from Henryk Górecki's Symphony No. 3, the sequence possesses an almost metaphysical quality. This sequence, an achievement in editing and special effects, is captured mostly in slow motion close-ups of passengers (embracing, praying, waiting in horror) interwoven with shots of the disintegration of the plane. Rafferty accurately comments that this sequence is a "furious kinetic vision of things ripping apart, of the end of the world inside a thin metal shell" (Rafferty, 122).

The final flashback sequence ends with a vision of Max departing for another world: the wreckage becomes a luminous passageway leading him to another dimension. It resembles images from Max's recent artworks, which Laura discovered in his studio: illuminated tunnels, labyrinths, visions commonly associated with the final passage to death. As portrayed in the illuminated fuselage, Max acquires an aura of mightiness. When he is about to leave the world, Laura's desperate attempts to rescue him are successful. Max wakes up from his strawberry-induced shock and, supposedly cured, expresses a desire to return to his previous safe life.

It is not difficult to see religious overtones in the film. Max, according to Weir, functions as an almost Christ-like figure, a savior, "The Good Samaritan," as the press labels him. Carla responds to his "preachings" as follows: "What you are telling me? There's no God but there's you?!" In many respects, Max is filmed in a God-like manner: his face is frequently "unnaturally" illuminated by natural sources of light—for instance, in a hotel when he is discovered by FBI agents or during the first meeting in his lawyer's office. The way Max is lit, the frequent shots of him in slow motion—for instance, when he crosses the street at a red light, onboard the plane when he helps his fellow passengers, and, above all, during the entire final flashback sequence—add an extra dimension to his worldly existence.

Max's identity is ambiguous. He is at once a buffoon and a savior, an angel and a monster, a merciless truth-teller, unafraid of hurting those who hold him dear, and someone who simply no longer cares. The press wants him to be a celebrity, his wife wants him back, his lawyer wants him to be cooperative, but Max wants none of this. Committed to telling only the truth, Max alienates his friends and family. For instance, his attitude toward the widow of his business partner and friend, Jeff Gordon (John de Lancie), who had also been

on the plane, is unsettling. On the one hand he comforts her and feels compassion for her. On the other, in his role of truth-teller, he cares only about himself and refuses to help her collect the insurance money she deserves.

The ambiguity surrounding Max is, to a large extent, due to the intricacy of Jeff Bridges's performance. He does not make Max an entirely likeable character, and his tense acting enhances the unsettling atmosphere of the film. Bridges has proven many times that he is capable of portraying multidimensional characters with psychological problems, trying to find meaning in a supposedly familiar world that has suddenly turned against them. His roles as a psychopath in *The Vanishing* (1993, George Sluizer) and a troubled father in *The American Heart* (1993, Martin Bell) are examples. Max, in Bridges's performance, undergoes a metamorphosis as he struggles to redefine himself and the world around him, which he no longer values.

As in all of his films, Weir pays a lot of attention to the look of *Fearless*. The crash sequence is among the most disturbing on film. The extensive use of slow motion adds an almost metaphysical atmosphere to the film.

Weir's dangerous tendency to oversentimentalize reappears in *Fearless*. The Christmas shopping sequence, in which Max buys a gift for his deceased father and Carla buys one for Bubble, is an example. Certainly, Weir tries to incorporate these sequences logically: for instance, in another scene Max tries to convince Carla that Bubble's death was not her fault and "re-creates" the plane crash in his Volvo with Carla in the backseat, holding a toolbox in her arms in place of a baby. He drives into a wall. Max ends up in the hospital, but Carla is relieved of her guilt.

Max's lawyer in the film, Brillstein (Tom Hulce), an amicable parody of the lawyer as vulture, claims that post-traumatic stress is to be blamed for his client's odd behavior. He hopes to negotiate for more money in damages. He also acts as lawyer for Carla and the wife of Max's dead friend. His presence introduces some comic relief into this film oriented toward tragedy.

Like Weir's earlier productions, *Fearless* does not belong to a single, identifiable genre. It shares with previous works an overwhelming sense of mysticism, the common thread that bonds Weir's films.

CHAPTER 12

Peter Weir's Personal Style

[Personal directors] are more interested in the way things look and feel and sound than in what they signify in general terms; more interested in mood than in narrative.

—Penelope Houston, *The Contemporary Cinema*

Despite occasional variations, Peter Weir's works possess visual and thematic unity. Furthermore, they are structured around one fundamental conflict: the clash of cultures.

Weir's films have a sensuous quality that affects feeling more than intellect. His filmic world evokes the enigmatic and the bizarre hidden beneath the visible, fragile surface of the rational. Fascinated by the domain between the unknown and reality, Weir carefully builds the tension between these two realms, trying to maintain an equilibrium between the rational and the irrational.[1] He devotes more time to building and maintaining a mood than to developing a story. He is more interested in exploring a mystery than in solving it.[2]

In spite of his refined, lush visual style, it is difficult to think of Weir as an innovative filmmaker. He is rather an imaginative, intuitive, hopelessly romantic mainstream auteur who, while cannibalizing popular culture, is not absorbed by it.

Most of Weir's films are distinguished by a dreamlike atmosphere and a visual symbolism that are capable of mesmerizing the viewer. They are built on sharp polarities, namely:

> Nature versus culture
> Myth versus reality
> The uncanny versus the familiar
> Innocence versus aggression
> New versus old
> The ideal versus the real
> Isolation versus openness

In the present pragmatic times, Weir may well be the last romantic among filmmakers. Thus, he sides with and idealizes the entries in the left-hand column at the expense of the others. These opposites find their visual equivalents in various forms:

1. Two worlds: Australia/overseas (*Picnic at Hanging Rock*, *Gallipoli*), West/East (*The Year of Living Dangerously*), America/Europe (*Green Card*).

2. Two communities: Aboriginal people/white Australians (*The Last Wave*), Amish/Americans (*Witness*), closed community/outsiders (*Homesdale*, *The Cars That Ate Paris*, *The Plumber*, *Witness*, *Dead Poets Society*).

3. Different groups or kinds of people: Youth/adults (*Michael*, *The Cars That Ate Paris*, *Picnic at Hanging Rock*, *Dead Poets Society*), strong personalities/vulnerable personalities (*The Mosquito Coast*, *Dead Poets Society*), people with different educational and cultural backgrounds (*Michael*, *Picnic at Hanging Rock*, *The Last Wave*, *The Plumber*, *Witness*, *Green Card*, *Fearless*).

While certain themes and means of visualizing them have persistently occupied Weir, he has also continued to evolve as he assimilates various influences and incorporates them into what is recognizable as his personal style. Most of his works transcend generic borders and some of them, particularly from his Australian period, do not belong to any definite genre. Though he works within many genres, his films are rather hybrids or reworkings of traditional formulas. One film, *Gallipoli*, marks an important point of departure in his artistic development. The major differences between the films made before and after what he calls his "graduation film" can be summarized as follows:

Before *Gallipoli*:	After *Gallipoli*:
Impressionistic narrative	Mainstream linear narrative
"Atmospheric" mood	Genre cinema
Spontaneous approach	Rational-professional approach
Australian themes	American themes

As indicated by these changes, Weir has gravitated toward mainstream cinema, nonetheless trying to maintain an uneasy balance between the pressures of commercial, big-studio productions and his personal vision. Before he left for the United States, Weir was an established filmmaker with his favorite themes and a recognizable style. In spite of his move to Hollywood, he has managed to preserve elements of his artistic integrity: in his style there are clear elements of both continuity and development. The noticeable change after *Gallipoli* is, one may argue, correlated not with a shift in Weir's thematic interests but with one in his method of visualizing them. Weir strengthens his narrative grasp; his new films introduce narrative patterns that are easier to follow and are less "atmospheric." To be sure, they belong to mainstream cinema, but they also contain Weir's familiar touches and themes: conflicts between incongruous cultures, protagonists' attempts to understand different cultures, characteristic visual images accompanied by his typical use of sound.

The principal interest of this filmmaker lies in observing clashes of cultures and the people involved. At the extreme, the ethnographic experience of the protagonist equals that of the viewer. Questions, however, are left without answers ("Some questions have answers, some not," goes the famous line from *Picnic at Hanging Rock*). Weir's characters are driven by forces they cannot comprehend. Confronted with a series of inexplicable events, they are forced to deal with spiritual forces and/or obscure incidents for which conventional modes of understanding are useless. The protagonists have to test their knowledge only to realize its futility. In their struggle against mysterious environments and incomprehensible occurrences, the protagonists of *Homesdale* (Mr. Malfrey) and *The Cars That Ate Paris* (Arthur Waldo) anticipate situations faced by Michael Fitzhubert in *Picnic at Hanging Rock,* David Burton in *The Last Wave,* and Jill Cowper in *The Plumber,* to name a few. They lose in their attempt to merge with another world and to understand its principles. (The only victor is the female protagonist, Jill, from *The Plumber.*)

A sense of menace is achieved by confronting filmic characters with the supernatural and the irrational within ordinary occurrences. These confrontations are, in a way, peripheral for Weir. It is the individuals involved in the confrontation who capture his attention. He explores their response to mystery. Unusual happenings, newly discovered cultures, and bizarre situations test the protagonists' knowledge and their systems of belief. History as well as politics is person-

alized. In this respect, Sue Mathews is right in stating that Weir's concern is with "personal rather than political morality" (Mathews, 70).

Western knowledge disappoints when confronted with the world of myths, dreams, and different cultural assumptions. The protagonist of most Weir films is an outsider who tries to overcome his inability to comprehend and communicate with an alien culture. In particular, Weir is interested in characters who suddenly find themselves outsiders—this is the initial premise of his works. What follows is a search for answers that are beyond rational comprehension. The protagonist's fascination with another culture is not accompanied by an ability to comprehend it. He must lose when faced with occurrences larger than his capabilities, different from his cultural assumptions. The mystery of Hanging Rock cannot be solved, the Aboriginal dream world is beyond the lawyer's understanding, the East (Indonesia) cannot be understood by Westerners, the closed Amish community, virtually unchanged since its beginnings, shuns contact with outsiders.

Most of Weir's early protagonists, as well as John Book in *Witness,* represent the world of logic and knowledge. These characters are mediators of and witnesses to the practices of another culture. They are rational heroes with rational professions: the lawyer, the reporter, the anthropologist, the police detective. They penetrate worlds different from their own experiences, attempt to rationalize what they see there, and finally (excluding *The Plumber*) fail. Irrational heroes dominate in Weir's recent films: the egomaniac adventurer Fox, the "Great Teacher" Keating, who values feelings more than knowledge, and the disoriented Max.

In the first group of works, the protagonist represents the viewer's (Western) logic, which clashes with a world ruled by its own principles; in the latter group, Western logic is a mirror that allows the protagonist to see himself. The hero acts against the viewer's pragmatic principles: Max behaves irrationally, Brontë and Georges break the law, and Keating promotes idealistic visions. As in earlier films, rationality is the target of Weir's anti-intellectualism. Whereas in the first group of films the rational protagonist is defeated by occurrences that are irrational from his (Western) perspective, in the second, irrational heroes lose to the forces of their rational environment, although, especially in *Dead Poets Society* and *Green Card,* their defeat contains a seed of future victory.

In many films the characters function as symbols rather than real-life figures. The schoolgirls from Appleyard College personify inno-

cence and repressed sexuality; the Aborigines, mystery and the natural world; the Anzacs, mythical bushmen transferred to World War I battlefields; the Amish, tradition and the rejection of modern civilization. As symbols, the characters are frequently deprived of individuality—for instance, the Aborigines in *The Last Wave.*

In emphasizing the inability of our culture to understand people from different cultural backgrounds, Weir has the tendency to romanticize "primitive people" (the Aborigines, the plumber, the Amish, etc.). Weir's anti-intellectualism, however, seems to derive from his attitude toward filmmaking: it is not in itself intellectual, but spontaneous. To be sure, opposing nature and culture, Weir always sides with nature. However, this does not restrain him from making some ironic comments (as in *Michael, The Plumber*), offering an overtly idealistic view (*The Last Wave, Witness, Dead Poets Society*), and introducing nature as both mysterious and sinister (*Picnic at Hanging Rock, The Last Wave*).

In Weir's world, it seems impossible to break out of the constraints of a given culture and successfully merge with another. He acknowledges the irreconcilability of cultures. The universal theme that appears in the conclusions to his films—separated worlds, the protagonists retreating to their tamed reality—confirms this assumption.

To a certain extent, the protagonists can be taken as personifications of Weir, his alter ego. They are usually his age and physical type, they are also getting older with him. For instance, Weir's early films are peopled with youthful characters entering their adulthood (the protagonist of *Michael,* Michael Fitzhubert, Archy Hamilton). Since *The Year of Living Dangerously* (and including *The Last Wave*) they have been professionals obsessed with their careers who witness corruption and lose their idealistic views. In recent films we have middle-aged characters who face midlife crisis (*Fearless*) and fight to bring the spirit of the past (the 1960s) to the present (the late 1980s) (*Dead Poets Society*).

Robert Winer, in a psychoanalytically oriented article, claims that there is a relation between Weir's personal growth and the thematics of his films. Weir's works, according to Winer, show a development from "witnessing" to "bearing witness," that is to say, "between taking in and giving forth, between passive registration and active testifying . . . between discovery and revelation."[3] Thus, Winer looks at Weir's five major films (from *Picnic at Hanging Rock* to *Witness*) as reflections of the director's personal development: from passive witnessing in his early works mirroring adolescent problems through a

coming of age (*Gallipoli*), to works dealing with contemporary concerns.

Though Weir is credited with an ability to create romantic tension, the motif of explicit sensual love, surprisingly, makes its entrance into his films rather late, with *The Year of Living Dangerously*. Romance, however, is usually unfulfilled. The lovers are separated by forces of history or politics (*The Year of Living Dangerously, Green Card*) or cultural difference (*Witness*).

In spite of the fact that Weir frequently portrays almost asexual figures and that sexuality commonly functions in his films on the spiritual level, some critics tend to look at his characters and the atmosphere created by his films in terms of repressed sexuality. Tania Modleski, for instance, claims that *Gallipoli* and *Picnic at Hanging Rock* are pervaded with "lyrical homoeroticism" and, furthermore, that *Dead Poets Society* is a vivid example of a film with repressed content "related to homoeroticism and gay sexuality" (Modleski, 137–38). Gary Hentzi sees Weir's "persistent interest in homosexuality" as implicit to several of his major films (Hentzi, 3).[4] These comments suggest, in my opinion, meanings rather marginal to Weir's work. The sensual atmosphere and the lack of explicit sexuality in most of his films cannot be taken automatically as another case of repressed, homosexual content, especially in the current age, in which much can be said openly.

Given the fact that Weir pays a great deal of attention to the visual quality of his films, it comes as no surprise that he focuses on meaningful images at the expense of dialogue. The images seem to be self-evident; his films even contain sequences without words (*Picnic at Hanging Rock, Witness, Dead Poets Society, Fearless*). As early as in his first critically recognized film, *Michael,* Weir cuts dialogue to a minimum and replaces it with rock music. The director tries to suggest meaning visually rather than through dialogue, which in some of his works (such as *The Last Wave, The Mosquito Coast*) weakens the impact of the film. In his best films (*Picnic at Hanging Rock, Gallipoli, Witness*) he favors nonverbal experience, with meaning implied through the combination of music and image. His films are very photogenic, they appeal to viewers' emotions and, characteristically, their impact is noticeable especially during the first viewing, in which feelings dominate logic.

In his early Australian films, Weir attempts to impede the perception of his works, rendering them more ambiguous and infusing

them with multiple implications; he "clears" his works of elements that would introduce clarity and suggests rather than delivers. He works around the subject and avoids ready answers. Thus, his early films resemble collages of images, and only from a certain distance can they offer the spectator an impression of delicate wholeness.

The best example of Weir's efforts to present his ideas in this "impressionistic" manner is *Picnic at Hanging Rock*. He does not employ traditional narrative with cause-effect relationships. Instead, he concentrates on the accompanying facts and skirts the story. This is the result of neither pure chance nor a lack of narrative competence but intention. For Weir, the narrative seems to be only a pretext through which to present a theme and create a mood. In *Picnic at Hanging Rock,* allegorical and mythical elements are more important than the story itself. Weir achieves a dreamlike atmosphere from the scraps of insinuated plots. He creates a world ruled by mystery. The protagonists move in this world as in a dream.

The power of images is intensified by the use of slow-motion sequences (*Picnic at Hanging Rock, The Last Wave, Gallipoli, Witness, Year of Living Dangerously, Dead Poets Society, Fearless*), soft-focus photography (mainly in *Picnic at Hanging Rock* and *Witness*), and superimpositions (*Picnic at Hanging Rock, Witness*). Intimacy is created by focusing on characters: their faces fill the screen, subjugated by the camera angles and movement. Further, the frequent use of zoom shots, in particular in *Fearless,* has the effect of flattening space, drawing attention to central characters. In collaboration with experienced directors of photography (Russell Boyd, John Seale, Allen Daviau, and others) Weir creates an oneiric, highly personal atmosphere by showing the supernatural, the uncanny, and the bizarre as they surface into daily life. He reinforces banal images and is not afraid to attempt a risky equilibrium between film art and kitsch.

To achieve his unique mood, Weir is ready not only to employ trivialized cinematic devices but also to use visual stereotypes related to a protagonist's image (as in the virginal girls in *Picnic at Hanging Rock*). The viewer may also find in his films banal symbolism (images of Miranda and the swan juxtaposed in *Picnic at Hanging Rock,* the cave in *Dead Poets Society,* birds as linking motifs in *Picnic* and *Poets*). He mixes "high art" and "popular art," influences from literature and painting with popular culture. Weir's originality, however, lies in the renewal and reinforcement of images degenerated into clichés. The recycled images look surprisingly refreshing in his films: he uses them as if invented for the first time.

Another important feature of Weir's cinema is his innovative use of the rural Australian landscape. Surprisingly, landscape doesn't play its expected role in his Gothic films. Instead, it is replaced by a house (*Homesdale*), an apartment (*The Plumber*), and an isolated country town (*The Cars That Ate Paris*). Reality is deformed, peopled with grotesque, ambiguous characters. The protagonist tries to survive in this bizarre environment. His only aim is to escape the nightmare and, like his counterpart in the horror genre, to restore normality.

In *Picnic at Hanging Rock* and *Gallipoli,* the landscape stands for Australia; it is a key to understanding Australia and defines the continent. The awe-inspiring landscape also performs a mythologizing function and is a source of mystery. Weir borrows heavily from the fine and literary arts. To depict the landscape effectively, he reinforces existing images and presents his version of Australia: a continent defined by its unique, threatening yet fascinating landscape and peopled by characters who dare to tame it.

The dominant role of nature in *Picnic at Hanging Rock* is replaced by history in *Gallipoli* and *The Year of Living Dangerously.* Nonetheless, Archy in *Gallipoli* seems to be led by the same unexplained magnetic force that takes Miranda into Hanging Rock. Both die and are transferred to a different realm to become the stuff of myths. Weir emphasizes this by employing slow motion for the girls' ascent up the rock and a freeze-frame of Archy during his decisive run on the Turkish trenches.

Weir's American films gradually move into an urban setting. After the pastoral landscape of *Witness,* peopled by the anachronistic Amish, *The Mosquito Coast* contrasts the ugliness of the rural American landscape with the dangerous beauty of the jungle. The landscape performs only an ornamental function in *Dead Poets Society.* In his urban American settings, Weir seems to be lost: presentation is superficial and unoriginal (*Green Card, Fearless*), unless the urban is there to help define a rural community (Philadelphia in *Witness*).

Music in Weir's films creates a sense of the inexplicable. It also stresses the incongruity of clashing worlds: the use of panpipe music and Beethoven in *Picnic at Hanging Rock,* the tribal drums and rock music in *The Plumber,* the musical score in *Witness,* which stresses the skewed temporality of the Amish. Music not only comments on the narrative but also creates a sense of the supernatural. Gheorghe Zamphir's panpipe music, employed in *Picnic at Hanging Rock,* serves as the best and, arguably, the most well-known example. In his inter-

views, Weir often emphasizes the importance of music to the atmosphere of his films: "Storytelling is my trade, my craft. But music is my inspiration; and my goal, my metaphor, to affect people like music. The images should float over you like music, and the experience should be beyond words" (McGilligan, 30).

The director is also known for the intelligent incorporation of well-known classical pieces into his films. In this respect, the use of diegetic and nondiegetic music in *Gallipoli* serves as a good example. The night before the disastrous slaughter at Gallipoli, Captain Burton listens to the tenor and baritone duet, "Au fond du temps saint," from Georges Bizet's *The Pearl Fishers,* on the battered old phonograph in his tent. Tomaso Albinoni's Adagio in G Minor for Strings and Organ, music full of pathos and sadness, introduced in the opening sequence, sets the mood for the film. Later, this musical motif appears so as to heighten the dramatic impact of the scene in which the Anzacs approach their destination. To these familiar classical pieces Jean-Michel Jarre's electronic music ("Oxygène") is added, which builds up the tension in the film's race sequences. The use of Albinoni and Bizet by Weir may undoubtedly be compared with Coppola's use of Wagner in *Apocalypse Now* (1979) and Kubrick's use of Strauss in *2001: A Space Odyssey* (1968).

As I stated earlier, Weir is not an innovative, groundbreaking auteur in cinema. Rather, he is a traditional filmmaker (with no disparagement intended) in both his treatment of narrative and in visual style. In his investigations of Australian mythology, Weir reconfirms the existing clichés and mythologies. He favors myth-enhancing narratives that reinforce rather than question and challenge existing order. Pat McGilligan states that Weir's films "do not vitriol or sting, instead they convey great muted feeling and passion. They are not likely to inflict pain, but count on them for strange foreboding and mesmerizing pleasure" (McGilligan, 23).

After *The Year of Living Dangerously,* as Weir shifted from Australian New Wave to Hollywood films, he deserted Australia for American settings and topics. His tendency toward clichéd and sentimental presentation was paralleled by a strengthening of narrative structure. The films that have followed *The Year of Living Dangerously,* more dramatically compact and controlled, have nonetheless continued to share thematic and stylistic features with their predecessors.

Weir's style is based on a structural opposition that is profoundly ethnographic: the clash between observer and observed, "us" and "them," Western rationality and Eastern/dreamtime/Amish mystery

organizes his films. We may sometimes see this idealism as naive and old-fashioned—it is only in Weir's cinema, presumably, that idealism has a chance when confronted with the victorious procession of pragmatism. Weir's poetic visual style and his passionate romantic sensibility make him one of the few members of the Dead Poets Society.

NOTES AND REFERENCES

After first reference here, all works are cited parenthetically in the text.

Chapter 1

1. Pat McGilligan, "Under Weir and Theroux," *Film Comment* 22, no. 6 (1986): 26.

2. Sue Mathews, *35mm Dreams: Conversations with Five Directors about the Australian Film Revival* (Melbourne: Penguin, 1984), 85.

3. David Stratton, *The Last New Wave: The Australian Film Revival* (Sydney: Angus and Robertson, 1980), 294.

4. See, for example, Graham Shirley and Brian Adams, *Australian Cinema: The First Eighty Years* (Sydney: Currency, 1983), 12-14 and 16-19.

5. Tom Weir [Tom Fitzgerald], "No Daydreams of Our Own: The Film as National Self-Expression," in *Australian Film Reader*, ed. Albert Morant and Tom O'Regan (1958; Sydney: Currency, 1985), 144.

6. John Baxter, *The Australian Cinema* (Sydney: Angus and Robertson, 1970).

7. Australian Film Commission, "Analysis of the Performance of Australian Films Since 1980" (1991), quoted from Elizabeth Jacka, "Film," *The Media in Australia: Industries, Texts, Audiences,* ed. Stuart Cunningham and Graeme Turner (Sydney: Allen and Unwin, 1993), 74.

8. Susan Dermody and Elizabeth Jacka, *Anatomy of a National Cinema,* vol. 2 of *The Screening of Australia* (Sydney: Currency, 1988), 28-37.

9. Michael Dempsey, "Inexplicable Feelings: An Interview with Peter Weir," *Film Quarterly* 33, no. 4 (1980): 5.

10. Richard White, *Inventing Australia: Images and Identity, 1688-1980* (Sydney: Allen and Unwin, 1981).

11. Ina Bertrand, " 'National Identity'/'National History'/'National Film': The Australian Experience," *Historical Journal of Film, Radio, and Television* 4, no. 2 (1984): 181.

Chapter 2

1. From Weir's comments in Bill Perkins, "Peter Weir's *Michael,*" *Mass Media Review* 7, no. 1 (1974): 12.

2. Brian McFarlane, "The Films of Peter Weir," insert in *Cinema Papers* 26 (1980a): 4.

3. Brian McFarlane and Tom Ryan, "Peter Weir: Towards the Centre" (an interview with Peter Weir), *Cinema Papers* 34 (1981): 325.

4. The film was released in the United States in a reedited, shortened (seventy-six minute), and partly redubbed version as *The Cars That Ate People*. Arthur turns into an American tourist on an exotic trip to Australia. Weir was not involved in these changes.

5. See, for instance, McFarlane's "The Films of Peter Weir," 6, and Stratton's *The Last New Wave*, 63. McFarlane believes that "*Cars* is satisfying because it integrates its elements—its narrative swiftness, its sharp observation of faces and places, its awareness that apparent ordinariness barely masks violence and terror—so as to make us privy to the horror which is at the heart of Weir's vision" (7).

6. Neil Rattigan, *Images of Australia: 100 Films of the New Australian Cinema* (Dallas: Southern Methodist University Press, 1991), 80-81.

7. Marsha Kinder, "*The Plumber*," *Film Quarterly* 33, no. 4 (1980): 17.

8. Peter Weir, *The Plumber: An Original Screenplay* (Adelaide: South Australian Film Corporation, 1978), 1-3.

9. Beverle Houston and Marsha Kinder, "The Losey-Pinter Collaboration," *Film Quarterly* 32 (1978): 17-30.

Chapter 3

1. Joan Lindsay, *Picnic at Hanging Rock*, was first published by Cheshire in 1967; all references in this text are to the Penguin 1970 edition. An intriguing new "final" chapter of the novel was revealed when Joan Lindsay died in 1984. Her former agent, John Taylor, stated that he was in possession of the last chapter, which was not to be released during Lindsay's lifetime. The final chapter appeared in the 1987 edition (on St. Valentine's Day) as *The Secret of Hanging Rock*, published by Angus and Robertson. The cover of the book depicts a reproduction of McCubbin's *The Lost Child*. The final chapter contains the "solution" to the mystery: the girls and Miss McCraw follow a small snake through a hole into a cave. Irma cannot follow her companions; the hole closes before her. Time stops at the rock. For more see Donald Barrett, "Picnicking with E. M. Forster, Joan Lindsay et al.," *Literature in North Queensland* 15, no. 1 (1987): 85.

2. Brian McFarlane, *Words and Images: Australian Novels into Film* (Melbourne: Heinemann and Cinema Papers, 1983), 43-45.

3. See Tom Inglis Moore, *Social Patterns in Australian Literature* (Berkeley: University of California Press, 1971), 99.

4. Brian Elliott, *The Landscape of Australian Poetry* (Melbourne: Cheshire, 1967), 67.

5. Rudolf Otto, *The Idea of the Holy: An Inquiry into the Non-Rational Factor in the Idea of the Divine and Its Relation to the Rational* (New York: Oxford University Press, 1958). Quoted from the Polish edition: *Świętość* (Warsaw: PiW, 1968), 43-46.

6. Glen Levis, *Australian Movies and the American Dream* (New York: Praeger, 1987), 87.

7. Geoffrey Dutton, "Gentlemen vs. Lairs," *Quadrant* 9, no. 1 (1965): 14.

8. David Myers, *Bleeding Battlers from Ironbark, Australian Myths in Fiction and Film: 1890s-1980s* (Rockhampton, Queensland: Capricornia Institute, 1987), 111.

9. Richard Combs, "*Picnic at Hanging Rock,*" *Monthly Film Bulletin* 43, no. 511 (1976): 197.

10. Ian Hunter, "Corsetway to Heaven: Looking Back to Hanging Rock," *Arena* 41 (1976): 11.

11. The term *genre* as applied by Dermody and Jacka to these films is justified because they possess unifying stylistic and thematic elements. See *Anatomy of a National Cinema,* 28-37.

12. Dermody and Jacka comment: "The AFC genre engages 'history' as a way of marketing a safe product, inviting genre nostalgia for a moment seen passing harmlessly under glass" (34).

13. The popularity of the AFC genre peaked in the late 1970s and early 1980s; it continued to exist mostly in television series, such as *The Anzacs* (1984), *Bodyline* (1984), *The Shiralee* (1986), *Vietnam* (1986), *Dirtwater Dynasty* (1987), and several other "high-quality" television films that were popular throughout the world.

14. Donald Barrett, "The Mythology of Pan and *Picnic at Hanging Rock,*" *Southerly* 3 (1982): 299-308.

15. Karelisa V. Hartigan, "Artemis in South Australia: Classical Allusions in *Picnic at Hanging Rock,*" *Classical and Modern Literature* 11, no. 1 (1990): 93-98.

16. Ann Crittenden, "*Picnic at Hanging Rock:* A Myth and Its Symbols," *Meanjin* 35, no. 2 (1976): 167-74.

17. Ford's painting, *Picnic Party at Hanging Rock Near Macedon,* in its way of presenting the British intrusion into an unfamiliar environment, has been both symptomatic and influential. Perhaps it is not a coincidence that Lindsay started her work on the novel soon after the painting was acquired in 1950. See Barrett 1987, 81, and his "Some Correspondence with Joan Lindsay," *Australian Literary Studies* 14, no. 1 (1989): 105.

18. See Joan Kirby, "Old Orders, New Lands: The Earth Spirit in *Picnic at Hanging Rock,*" *Australian Literary Studies* 8, no. 3 (1978): 255-68; and Barrett 1987, 79-86.

19. John Scheckter, "The Lost Child in Australian Fiction," *Modern Fiction Studies* 27, no. 1 (1981): 62. One could argue Scheckter's point by saying that the myth of the lost child is universal; for example, innumerable versions of the Hansel and Gretel story.

20. For example, Brian McFarlane, "Horror and Suspense," in *The New Australian Cinema,* ed. Scott Murray (Melbourne: Nelson, 1980b). In the same book Adrian Martin considers *Picnic at Hanging Rock* and *The Last*

Wave as "fantasy films"; see 97-100 and 106-9. See also Charles Derry, "More Dark Dreams: Some Notes on the Recent Horror Film," in *American Horrors: Essays on the Modern American Horror,* ed. Gregory A. Waller (Urbana and Chicago: University of Illinois Press, 1987), 171-72.

21. Jan Dawson, "Picnic under Capricorn," *Sight and Sound* 45, no. 2 (1976): 83.

Chapter 4

1. Piotr Zawojski, "Świat jako projekcja świadomości: *Ostatnia fala*" (World as a Projection of Consciousness), *Szwenk* 3 (1985): 11-22.

2. Adrian Martin, "Fantasy," in *New Australian Cinema,* 106.

3. Weir claims that his interest lies "in those unknown areas" and "not so much in finding neat endings. There are no answers, there is no ending." Quoted in David Stratton, *The Last New Wave: The Australian Film Revival* (Sydney: Angus and Robertson, 1980), 77.

4. See C. G. Jung, *Psychological Reflections: A New Anthology of His Writings, 1905-1961,* ed. Jolande Jacobi (Princeton: Princeton University Press, 1973).

5. Terry Dowling and George Mannix, "Peter Weir: Master of Unease," *Science Fiction: A Review of Speculative Literature* 3, no. 1 (1980): 14.

6. Weir stresses the importance of David Gulpilil's and Nandjiwarra Amagula's contributions to the final version of the film. See Mathews, 96-98.

7. Andrew Pike, "Aboriginals in Australian Feature Films," *Meanjin* 4 (1977): 592-99.

8. Surprisingly, the same practice was employed in *Journey Out of Darkness,* directed by James Trainor, a 1967 film about a white policeman escorting to trial an Aborigine accused of murder. The role of the Aboriginal tracker is played by a white actor, Ed Devereaux, the role of the killer by a Sri Lankan-born singer, Kamahl. See Shirley and Adams, 228-29.

9. Catriona Moore and Stephen Muecke, "Racism and the Representation of Aborigines in Film," *Australian Journal of Cultural Studies* 2, no. 1 (1984): 39.

10. Graeme Turner, "Breaking the Frame: The Representation of Aborigines in Australian Film," in *Aboriginal Culture Today,* ed. Anna Rutherford (Melbourne: Dangaroo Press—Kunapipi, 1988), 140.

11. See Helen Daniel's illuminating discussion, "The Aborigine in Australian Fiction: Stereotype to Archetype?" *Modern Fiction Studies* 27, no. 1 (1981): 45-60.

Chapter 5

1. Claudia and Peter Fonda-Bonardi, "The Birth of a Nation: An Interview with Peter Weir," *Cineaste* 11, no. 4 (1982): 42.

2. Henry Lawson, "Song of the Dardanelles," *A Literary Heritage: Henry Lawson* (Richmond, Victoria: Octopus, 1988), 155.

3. Phillip Adams, "Two Views," *Cinema Papers* 44-45 (1984): 71.

4. J. Eddy and D. Schreuder, eds., *The Rise of Colonial Nationalism* (Sydney: Allen and Unwin, 1988), 153.

5. Bill Gammage, "Anzac," in *Intruders in the Bush: The Australian Quest for Identity,* ed. John Carroll (Melbourne: Oxford University Press, 1982), 57.

6. Jane Freebury, "Screening Australia—*Gallipoli:* A Study of Nationalism on Film," *Media Information Australia* 43 (1987): 5.

7. George Seddon, "The Evolution of Perceptual Attitudes," in *Man and Landscape in Australia: Towards an Ecological Vision,* ed. George Seddon and Mari Davis (Canberra: Australian Government Publishing Service, 1976), 13.

8. John Tulloch, *Legends on the Screen: The Narrative Film in Australia, 1919–1929* (Sydney: Currency, 1981).

9. Russel Ward, *The Australian Legend* (Melbourne: Oxford University Press, 1974), 238-59.

10. Brian McFarlane, *Australian Cinema, 1970–1985* (Melbourne: William Heinemann Australia, 1987), 47.

11. Henry Lawson, "Ballad of the Cornstalk," in *The Australian Experience of War,* ed. John Laird (Darlinghurst: Mead and Beckett, 1988), 18-19.

12. See a discussion in David Buchbinder's "Mateship, *Gallipoli,* and the Eternal Masculine," in *Representation, Discourse, and Desire: Contemporary Australian Culture and Critical Theory,* ed. Patrick Fuery (London: Longman Cheshire, 1994), 115-37.

13. Henry Lawson, *Poetical Works* (Sydney: Angus and Robertson, 1964), 103.

14. Tom Inglis Moore, *Social Patterns in Australian Literature* (Berkeley: University of California Press, 1971), 99.

15. Bill Gammage, *The Broken Years* (Ringwood, Victoria: Penguin, 1974).

16. See K. S. Inglis, *C. E. W. Bean: Australian Historian* (Brisbane: University of Queensland Press, 1970). Bean's work, *The Story of Anzacs from the Outbreak of War to the End of the First Phase of the Gallipoli Campaign,* has been described by a British reviewer as the "Iliad and Odyssey of Australia," (quoted in Inglis, 20).

17. William J. Palmer, *The Films of the Seventies: A Social History* (Metuchen, N.J.: Scarecrow, 1987), 244.

18. Sylvia Lawson, "*Gallipoli:* Picnic at the Pyramids," *Filmnews,* November-December 1981, 11.

19. Anne B. Hutton, ed., *The First Australian History and Film Conference Papers* (Sydney: Australian Film and Television School, 1982), 215.

20. A. D. Hope, *Selected Poems* (Sydney: Angus and Robertson, 1973), 13.

21. Phillip Adams, "*Gallipoli,*" *Age* (Melbourne), 22 August 1981, 11.

22. Louise Merryweather, ed., *Peter Weir's Film of Gallipoli: Film Study Guide* (Melbourne: Applied Media Resources, Education Department of Victoria, 1981).

23. Anne B. Hutton, "Nationalism in Australian Cinema," *Cinema Papers* 26 (1980): 153.

24. Quoted from Mary Eagle, "Painting an Australian Identity," in *Intruders in the Bush,* 189.

Chapter 6

1. C. J. Koch, *The Year of Living Dangerously* (1978; Melbourne: Thomas Nelson, 1982), 85; all references are to the 1982 paperback edition.

2. Susan McKernan, "C. J. Koch's Two-Faced Vision," *Meanjin* 44, no. 4 (1985): 434.

3. D. M. Roskies, "A View of Asia from Down Under: The Politics of Re-Presentation in *The Year of Living Dangerously,*" *World Literature Written in English* 29, no. 2 (1989): 36.

4. See particularly Carolyn Durham, "*The Year of Living Dangerously:* Can Vision Be a Model for Knowledge?" *Jump Cut* 30 (1985a): 6-7, and her "Visual Politics in *The Year of Living Dangerously:* To See or Not to See," *Perspectives on Contemporary Literature* 11 (1985b): 117-25. See also James Roy MacBean, "Watching the Third World Watchers," *Film Quarterly* 37, no. 3 (1984): 3-13.

5. For instance, B. N. Balajee, "The Fusion of Myth and Topicality in Christopher Koch's *The Year of Living Dangerously,*" *Literary Criterion* 23, no. 3 (1988): 34-37, and Hena Maes-Jelinek, "History and the Mythology of Confrontation in *The Year of Living Dangerously,*" *Kunapipi* 8, no. 1 (1986): 27-35.

6. Margaret Yong, "Explorations in the Heart of Darkness: Turning Landscape into Art in *Slipstream* and *The Year of Living Dangerously,*" in *Discharging the Canon: Cross-Cultural Readings in Literature,* ed. Peter Hyland (Singapore: Singapore University Press, 1986), 29.

7. The narrator of the novel, Cookie, is an enigmatic father confessor to his fellow journalists, who may be easily taken as the author in disguise— Koch is the obvious Germanization of "Cook." His role is to record events and to comment on them. It is a passive, neutral voice, left mostly uncharacterized by Koch.

8. For instance, Neil Rattigan's comments expressed in his insightful book on the New Australian Cinema, *Images of Australia,* 325-26.

Chapter 7

1. For instance, the Australian critic Sandra Hall calls *Witness* "the most elegantly constructed of all Weir's films," in which, while reworking the American formula, he retains his familiar features: "his eye for transfixing image, his feeling for ritual, his fascination with innocence and the sense of

occasion with which he can enliven the everyday." Sandra Hall, "US Hit Bears Witness to Weir's Genius," *Bulletin*, 7 May 1985, 86.

2. Richard Combs, "*Witness*," *Monthly Film Bulletin* 52, no. 616 (1985): 167.

3. Robert Phillip Kolker, "Gun Lore: *Witness*," *Cinema Papers*, May 1985, 82.

4. See a study by John A. Hostetler, *Amish Society* (1963; Baltimore and London: Johns Hopkins University Press, 1980).

5. Wayne J. McMullen, "A Rhetorical Analysis of Peter Weir's *Witness*" (Ph.D. diss., Pennsylvania State University, 1989), 279.

6. John P. McGowan, "Looking at the (Alter)natives: Peter Weir's *Witness, Chicago Review* 35, no. 2 (1986): 12.

7. The term *utopia*, first employed by Sir Thomas More (1478-1535), describes a place of ideal perfection, a hypothetical construct. Utopia does not allow for the introduction of something new—it is a crime against perfection. As McGowan notices, Eli's condemnation of dancing to Sam Cooke's song threatens our sympathy with the Amish culture because of its "tyrannical insistence on the strict fidelity of its individual members to its choices" (McGowan, 43).

8. A similar point is taken up by Combs in his review of *Witness*. He speaks of this "film's charming quality, the playing of Harrison Ford and Kelly McGillis—or the meeting cute of Dirty Harry and Grace Kelly from the Zinnemann film." Combs, "*Witness*," 167.

9. As Combs accurately observes: "The dream ends when the men with guns move in." Combs, "*The Mosquito Coast*," *Monthly Film Bulletin* 54, no. 637 (1987): 53.

10. Linda Hansen, "*Witness*: A New Image of Nonviolence in Popular Film," *Journal of Popular Film and Television* 14, no. 3 (1986): 136-41.

11. "Dialogue on Film: Peter Weir," *American Film* 11, no. 5 (1986): 14.

12. McGowan comments that "looking at other cultures might stir the imagination, but the alternatives to our own practices formulated in response to that encounter require the words of negation, the words that can offer visions of absent possibilities" (McGowan, 41).

Chapter 8

1. Paul Theroux, *The Mosquito Coast* (Boston: Houghton Mifflin, 1982).

2. Samuel Coale, *Paul Theroux* (Boston: Twayne, 1987), 115.

3. Terrence Rafferty, "*The Mosquito Coast*," *Nation*, 13 December 1986, 684.

4. Stanley Kauffmann, "*The Mosquito Coast*," *New Republic*, 22 December 1986, 26.

5. Steven R. Luebke, "Self Dark Circle: The Home-Founding Journey in Paul Theroux's *The Mosquito Coast* and Stephen Minot's *Ghost Images*," *Critique: Studies in Contemporary Fiction* 30, no. 4 (1989): 227.

6. Bruce Bawer, "Life with Father," *American Spectator* 20, no. 2 (February 1987): 34.

7. The irony of this final scene is more explicit in the novel. Fox and some birds (vultures and pelicans) are fighting over garbage. "Know why I hate scavengers?" he asks. "Because they remind me of human beings." In the book's powerful climax, the hero is attacked by vultures and one rips out his tongue! (Theroux, 309-10).

8. Nora Lee, "*Mosquito Coast:* A Jungle Utopia Gone Awry," *American Cinematographer* 68, no. 2 (1987): 61-62.

9. Gary Hentzi stresses that the result of this new approach is a film with a styleless style, "just another Hollywood movie with an unsalable theme." Hentzi, "Peter Weir and the Cinema of New Age Humanism," *Film Quarterly* 44, no. 2 (1990-91): 11.

Chapter 9

1. Bruce Bawer, "Poetry in Motion," *American Spectator* 22, no. 8 (August 1989): 40.

2. Robert B. Heilman, "The Great-Teacher Myth," *American Scholar,* Summer 1989, 419. In his illuminating and amusing essay, Heilman goes far beyond the realm of the film and discusses the Keating characters in contemporary academia.

3. John Simon, "The Red, Red Robin Comes Blabbin' Along," *National Review,* 15 September 1989, 54.

4. Pamela A. Rooks, "Woo Who? Exclusion of Otherness in *Dead Poets Society,*" *Australian Journal of Communication* 18, no. 2 (1991): 75-83.

5. Harry M. Geduld, "Seize the Day?" *Humanist,* September/October 1989, 41.

6. John Carroll, "*Dead Poets Society* and Our Times," *Quadrant* 34, no. 3 (1990): 39.

7. Stanley Kauffmann, "Boys' Lives," *New Republic,* 26 June 1989, 26.

8. Pauline Kael, "Stonework," *New Yorker,* 26 June 1989, 71.

9. Barbra Luby, "*Dead Poets Society,*" *Filmnews* 19, no. 6 (1989): 13.

10. Pauline Kael quoted in *The Imaginary Industry: Australian Film in the Late 80s,* ed. Susan Dermody and Elizabeth Jacka (Sydney: AFTRS Publications, 1988), 68. Special Issue of *Media Information Australia* 50 (1988).

11. The superficiality of Weir's film distresses Evan Carton: "Carpe diem is not revolutionary poetry but America's premier cliché. In the current speech of the sons, it means 'go for it.' In the controlling discourse of the fathers, it is 'business as usual.' " Evan Carton, "Better Dead Than Read: The Society of Poets," *Tikkun* 4, no. 6 (1989): 67.

12. For Tania Modleski, the repressed content of this film is related to homosexuality, and, accordingly, Todd reveals signs of "sexual identity crisis." She believes "a more honest version of the film" would have shown Todd "struggling to come to terms with being gay in a heterosexual, homosocial

environment." Her comment seems to overlook the essence of the film at the expense of sexual politics narrowly understood. See Tania Modleski, *Feminism without Women: Culture and Criticism in a "Postfeminist" Age* (New York and London: Routledge, 1991), 137–45.

Chapter 10

1. Katherine Tulich, "Peter Weir" (interview), *Cinema Papers* 80 (1990): 8.

2. Verina Glaessner, "*Green Card,*" *Monthly Film Bulletin* 58, no. 686 (1991): 80.

Chapter 11

1. Rafael Yglesias, *Fearless* (New York: Warner Bros., 1993).

2. John Simon, "Believe It Who Will," *National Review,* 29 November 1993, 69–71.

3. See, for instance, *Film Comment* 30, no. 1 (1994). Richard Jameson ranks *Fearless* in group "II" with such prominent films as Spielberg's *Schindler's List* and Kieślowski's *Trois Couleurs: Bleu* (44). Kathleen Murphy places the film among the ten best with *Short Cuts* by Altman and, again, films by Kieślowski and Spielberg (45).

4. See comments on Daviau's work and his insights in Bob Fisher's "*Fearless* Explores Emotional Aftermath of Fateful Flight," *American Cinematographer* 74, no. 11 (1993): 40–51.

5. Terrence Rafferty, "After the Crash," *New Yorker,* 25 October 1993, 121.

Chapter 12

1. Sandra Hall notes that Weir "is a genius for juxtaposing the odd with the ordinary in a gleeful belief that things are never just as they seem." Sandra Hall, "US Hit Bears Witness to Weir's Genius," *Bulletin,* 7 May 1985, 86.

2. Weir states: "Most of my films have been left incomplete with the viewer as the final participant: I don't like the didactic approach. One is constantly left wondering and I love when that's done to me in a film" (Mathews, 107).

3. Robert Winer, "Witnessing and Bearing Witness: The Ontogeny of Encounter in the Films of Peter Weir," in *Images in Our Souls: Cavell, Psychoanalysis, and Cinema,* ed. Joseph H. Smith and William Kerrigan (Baltimore: Johns Hopkins University Press, 1987), 84.

4. Hentzi points out the sensual homoerotic atmosphere of *Picnic at Hanging Rock, Gallipoli* (but taken without its cultural "mateship" context), *The Year of Living Dangerously* (Guy Hamilton and Billy Kwan, however, form a different kind of relationship), and *Dead Poets Society* ("Weir has filled the screen with images of strikingly attractive young men; yet no mention is made of illicit love") (3). Later, however, he admits that this motif is "a figure for a larger and considerably more ambiguous set of issues" (4).

SELECTED BIBLIOGRAPHY

Primary Sources
INTERVIEWS

Dempsey, Michael. "Inexplicable Feelings: An Interview with Peter Weir." *Film Quarterly* 33, no. 4 (1980): 2-11. An important, lengthy interview with many insightful comments, in particular on *Picnic at Hanging Rock*.

"Dialogue on Film: Peter Weir." *American Film* 11, no. 5 (1986): 13-15. Weir's films are discussed as crossing boundaries between people and cultures.

Dowling, Terry, and George Mannix. "Peter Weir—Master of Unease (An Interview with Peter Weir)." *Science Fiction—A Review of Speculative Literature* 3, no. 1 (1980): 7-27. A significant, wide-ranging discussion on the speculative and imaginative aspect of Weir's filmmaking.

Fonda-Bonardi, Claudia, and Peter. "The Birth of a Nation: An Interview with Peter Weir." *Cineaste* 11, no. 4 (1982): 41-42. A short but valuable interview focusing on *Gallipoli*.

"I Felt Somehow I Was Touching History." *Literature/Film Quarterly* 9, no. 4 (1981): 213-17. A brief interview on the making of *Gallipoli*.

Magill, Marcia. "Peter Weir: An Interview." *Films in Review* 32, no. 8 (1981): 474-79. Weir discusses *Gallipoli,* his career, and future plans.

Mathews, Sue. "Peter Weir." In *35mm Dreams: Conversations with Five Directors about the Australian Film Revival,* 69-114. Melbourne: Penguin, 1984. A major interview covering Weir's entire life and career in great detail.

McFarlane, Brian, and Tom Ryan. "Peter Weir: Towards the Centre." *Cinema Papers* 34 (1981): 323-28. An essential interview with many insights into Weir's films.

McGilligan, Pat. "Under Weir and Theroux." *Film Comment* 6 (1986): 23-32. A significant, lengthy interview covering Weir's entire career.

Tulich, Katherine. "Peter Weir: Interview." *Cinema Papers* 80 (1990): 6-10. A casual, informative discussion focusing on Weir's American works and experiences.

Secondary Sources
BOOKS WITH REFERENCES TO WEIR

Beilby, Peter, and Ross Lansell, eds. *Australian Motion Picture Yearbook 1983.* Melbourne: 4 Seasons and Cinema Papers, 1982. Contains a profile of Weir by Brain McFarlane, "Peter Weir," 237-48.

Bertrand, Ina, and Diane Collins. *Government and Film in Australia.* Sydney: Currency, 1981.

Dermody, Susan, and Elizabeth Jacka. *Anatomy of a Film Industry.* Vol. 1 of *The Screening of Australia.* Sydney: Currency, 1987.

————. *Anatomy of a National Cinema.* Vol. 2 of *The Screening of Australia.* Sydney: Currency, 1988.

————, eds. *The Imaginary Industry: Australian Film in the Late 80s.* Sydney: AFTRS Publications, 1989. (Special issue of *Media Information Australia,* no. 50 [1988].) Essential studies tracing the economic, political, and cultural forces behind the Australian film renaissance. Many valuable insights into Weir's films.

Gammage, Bill, David Williamson, and Peter Weir. *The Story of Gallipoli.* Ringwood: Penguin, 1981. About the making of the film. Includes Williamson's screenplay.

Green, Cliff. *"Picnic at Hanging Rock": A Film.* Melbourne: Cheshire, 1975. The screenplay and material about the film.

Hall, Sandra. *Critical Business: The New Australian Cinema in Review.* Adelaide: Rigby, 1985. Contains reviews of Weir's Australian films.

Haltof, Marek. *Kino Australii: O ekranowej konstrukcji Australii* (Australian Cinema: On the Screen Construction of Australia). Łódź, Poland: Film and Television School, 1996. A study on New Wave Australian cinema, in particular on the questions of "Australianess." Contains lengthy chapters on *Picnic at Hanging Rock* and on the poetics of Weir's cinema.

Kelley, William, and Earl W. Wallace. *Witness.* New York: Pocket Books, 1985. The novelization of the screenplay.

Lewis, Glen. *Australian Movies and the American Dream.* New York: Praeger, 1987. A detailed coverage of Australian feature films with reference to U.S. connection. Discusses several Weir films.

Malone, Peter. *In Black and White and Colour: Aborigines in Australian Feature Films—A Survey.* Richmond, Victoria: Spectrum, 1987. Contains a chapter on *The Last Wave.*

McFarlane, Brian. *Australian Cinema 1970-1985.* Melbourne: Heinemann Australia, 1987. Well-illustrated thematic and stylistic study of Australian cinema. Many references to Weir's films.

————. *Words and Images: Australian Novels into Film.* Melbourne: Heinemann and Cinema Papers, 1983. Examines the relationship between literature and film. Illuminating chapters on *Picnic at Hanging Rock* and *The Year of Living Dangerously.*

McFarlane, Brian, and George Mayer. *New Australian Cinema: Sources and Parallels in American and British Film.* Cambridge: Cambridge University Press, 1992. Provides a discussion on *Picnic at Hanging Rock, The Last Wave,* and *Witness.*

Merryweather, Louise, ed. *Peter Weir's Film of Gallipoli: Film Study Guide.* Melbourne: Applied Resources, Education Department of Victoria, 1981. A lengthy study guide designed for use in secondary schools.

Moran, Albert, and Tom O'Regan, eds. *The Australian Screen*. Melbourne: Penguin, Australia, 1989. An enticing survey of Australian film. References to Weir's films.

Murray, Scott, ed. *Australian Film 1978-1992*. Melbourne: Oxford University Press, 1993. Meticulously researched resource book. Contains reviews of *Gallipoli, The Year of Living Dangerously*, and *Green Card*.

———. *The New Australian Cinema*. Melbourne: Nelson and Cinema Papers, 1980. Weir's earlier films are discussed, particularly in chapters written by Adrian Martin and Brian McFarlane.

Myers, David. *Bleeding Battlers from Ironbark: Australian Myths in Fiction and Film, 1890s-1980s*. Rockhampton, Queensland: Capricornia Institute, 1987. This lively book contains chapters on *Picnic at Hanging Rock* and *Gallipoli*.

Peeters, Theo. *Peter Weir and His Films: A Critical Bibliography*. Melbourne: Australian Film Institute Research and Information, 1983. An exhaustive listing of all printed material concerning Weir's career prior to 1982.

Pike, Andrew, and Ross Cooper. *Australian Film 1900-1977: A Guide to Feature Film Production*. Melbourne: Oxford University Press and the Australian Film Institute, 1980. An indispensable book on Australian cinema. Comments on *Michael, Homesdale, Picnic at Hanging Rock,* and *The Last Wave*.

Rattigan, Neil. *Images of Australia: 100 Films of the New Australian Cinema*. Dallas: Southern Methodist University Press, 1991. An essential book on New Australian Cinema. An excellent discussion on Weir's Australian films in the broad social and cultural context of the Australian New Wave cinema.

Reade, Eric. *History and Heartburn: The Saga of Australian Film, 1896-1978*. Sydney: Harper and Row, 1979. References to Weir films.

Shaffer, Kay. *Women and the Bush: Forces of Desire in the Australian Cultural Tradition*. Sydney: Cambridge University Press, 1988. A feminist approach to Australian culture. Contains a lively discussion on *Picnic at Hanging Rock*.

Shiach, Don. *The Films of Peter Weir: Visions of Alternative Realities*. London: C. Letts, 1993. An informative discussion of Weir's films in the light of the auteur theory. The first book fully devoted to Weir's cinema.

Shirley, Graham, and Brian Adams. *Australian Cinema: The First Eighty Years*. Sydney: Angus and Robertson/Currency, 1983. An indispensable book on Australian cinema from its pioneering days to 1975. References to Weir's early films.

Stratton, David. *The Avocado Plantation: Boom and Bust in the Australian Film Industry*. Sydney: Macmillan, 1990. A personal account of the Australian film industry between 1980 and 1990. Many references to Weir.

———. *The Last New Wave: The Australian Film Revival*. Sydney: Angus and Robertson, 1981. Discusses Weir's films in chapter 5, "Mystery and Imagination." Personal, detailed comments on early Weir's films.

Turner, Graeme. *National Fictions: Literature, Film, and the Construction of Australian Narrative.* Sydney: Allen and Unwin, 1986. An important work, the first book in Australian studies to deal with the cultural construction of narratives. References to Weir.

White, David. *Australian Movies to the World: The International Success of Australian Films since 1970.* Melbourne: Fontana Australia and Cinema Papers, 1984. Includes Weir's profile by Debi Enker and many references to his career.

Williamson, Dugald. "Local Consumption: 'Peter Weir,' " chapter 5 of *Authorship and Criticism,* 64–84. Sydney: Local Consumption Publications, 1989. Through a case study of some films directed by Weir, Williamson demonstrates the main differences between author-based and alternative forms of criticism.

Winer, Robert. "Witnessing and Bearing Witness: The Ontogeny of Encounter in the Films of Peter Weir." In *Images in Our Souls: Cavell, Psychoanalysis, and Cinema,* edited by Joseph H. Smith and William Kerrigan, 82–108. Baltimore: Johns Hopkins University Press, 1987. Looks at Weir's five major films (from *Picnic at Hanging Rock* to *Witness*) and provides an analysis of the relation between Weir's personal growth and the thematics of his films.

ARTICLES ON (OR WITH REFERENCE TO) WEIR

Brennan, Richard. "Peter Weir." *Cinema Papers,* January 1974, 16–17. Discusses the early stage of Weir's career.

Clancy, Jack. "Music in the Films of Peter Weir." *Journal of Australian Studies* 41 (1994): 24–34. A major article on the use of music in Weir's films.

Collier, Gordon, and Geoffrey Davis. "The Iconography of Landscape in Australian Film." *Australian and New Zealand Studies in Canada* 6 (1991): 27–41. An illuminating discussion on the role of landscape in Australian films. The landscape in *Gallipoli.*

Crofts, Stephen. "Shifting Paradigms in the Australian Historical Film." *East-West Film Journal* 5, no. 2 (1991): 1–15. Contains a discussion on *Gallipoli.*

Gibson, Ross. "Camera Natura: Landscape in Australian Feature Films." *Framework* 22–23 (1983): 47–51. Discusses Australian landscape as the leitmotif and ubiquitous character in Australian films.

Haltof, Marek. "Etnograficzne przeżycia: Peter Weir i jego filmy" (Ethnographic Experiences: Peter Weir and His Films). *Film na Świecie* 381 (1991): 5–16. A lengthy overview focusing on Weir's personal style.

————. "O kinie onirycznym Petera Weira" (On Peter Weir's Oneiric Cinema). *Studia Filmoznawcze X,* edited by Jan Trzynadlowski (1991): 231–43. Discusses the dreamlike aspect of Weir's cinema.

Hentzi, Gary. "Peter Weir and the Cinema of New Age Humanism." *Film Quarterly* 44, no. 2 (1990/1991): 2–12. A major article focusing on Weir's

development. Emphasis is on an exploration of discreet sexuality and spiritual forces in Weir's cinema.

McFarlane, Brian. "The Films of Peter Weir." Insert in *Cinema Papers* 26 (1980): 24 pp. A comprehensive and lengthy treatment of Weir's early films, with an emphasis on thematics.

UNPUBLISHED MANUSCRIPTS ON WEIR

Corum, Everett Eugene. "Tantalizing Ambiguity: The Cinema of Peter Weir." Ph.D. diss. University of Kansas, 1990. Describes the content of Weir's films, their basic narrative structures and thematic concerns.

Haltof, Józef Marek. "Film and Dream: The Films of Peter Weir." M.A. thesis. Flinders University, Adelaide, Australia, 1988. Discusses the oneiric aspect of Weir's cinema.

McMullen, Wayne Joseph. "A Rhetorical Analysis of Peter Weir's *Witness*." Ph.D. diss. Pennsylvania State University, 1989. This well-researched and -executed study examines the rhetorical form of the film and the implied response of the viewer.

REVIEWS, ARTICLES, AND PARTS OF BOOKS ON INDIVIDUAL FILMS
Gothic Films

Brown, Geoff. "*The Cars That Ate Paris*." *Sight and Sound* 44, no. 3 (1975): 192.

Clancy, Jack. "*The Plumber*." *Cinema Papers* 23 (1979): 569-70.

[Flaus, John.]. "*The Cars That Ate Paris*." *Cinema Papers*, July 1974: 274-75.

Glenn, Gordon, and Scott Murray. "*The Cars That Ate Paris*: Production Report." *Cinema Papers*, January 1974: 18-26.

Kinder, Marsha. "*The Plumber*." *Film Quarterly* 32, no. 4 (1979): 17-21. An excellent review of the film.

Nicholls, Rod. "Peter Weir." *Lumiere* 21 (1973): 4-7. A valuable discussion on Weir's early short films.

Perkins, Bill. "Peter Weir's *Michael*" [includes "Notes on the Making of *Michael* by the Director Peter Weir"]. *Mass Media Review* 7, no. 1 (1974): 12-17. *Michael* as a teaching tool in secondary schools.

Strick, Philip. "*The Cars That Ate Paris*." *Monthly Film Bulletin* 496 (1974): 101-2.

Wilson, David. "*The Cars That Ate Paris*." *Sight and Sound* 44, no. 3 (1975): 192-93.

Picnic at Hanging Rock

Combs, Richard. "*Picnic at Hanging Rock*." *Monthly Film Bulletin* 43, no. 511 (1976): 196-97.

Craven, Jenny. "*Picnic at Hanging Rock*." *Films and Filming* 23, no. 3 (1976): 31-32.

Crittenden, Anne. "*Picnic at Hanging Rock*: A Myth and Its Symbols." *Meanjin* 35, no. 2 (1976): 167-74. An analysis of the film's key images with

respect to the confrontation of civilization and nature that occur in the film.

Dawson, J. "Picnic under Capricorn." *Sight and Sound* 45, no. 2 (1976): 83.

Garbicz, Adam. "Kryształ Petera Weira" (The Crystal of Peter Weir). *Kino* 7 (1979): 48-53. A sympathetic attempt at analysis of the film.

Ginnane, A. I., and Scott Murray. "Producing *Picnic:* Pat Lovell." *Cinema Papers,* March/April 1976: 298-301.

Haltof, Marek. "A Dream within a Dream." *S—European Journal for Semiotic Studies* 2, no. 1 (1990): 79-93. Discusses the oneiric aspect of *Picnic at Hanging Rock* and *The Last Wave.*

Hartigan, Karelisa V. "Artemis in South Australia: Classical Allusions in *Picnic at Hanging Rock.*" *Classical and Modern Literature: A Quarterly* 11, no. 1 (1990): 93-98. Links myth and film and looks for echoes and reflections of the classical world and its traditions in the structure of the film.

Hunter, Ian. "Corsetway to Heaven: Looking back at *Picnic at Hanging Rock.*" *Cinema Papers,* March-April, 1976, 371. Also published in *Arena* 41 (1976): 9-12. A short, dissenting yet important look at Weir's film, highly critical of its superficiality.

Jankun, Mariola. "*Piknik pod Wiszącą Skałą:* O mitycznej przestrzeni dzieła" (*Picnic at Hanging Rock:* On the Mythological Space of the Work). *Kino* 4 (1984): 37-41. Focuses on the mythological dimension of Weir's film.

Milne, Tom. "*Picnic at Hanging Rock.*" *Sight and Sound* 45, no. 4 (1976): 257.

Murray, Scott. "*Picnic at Hanging Rock.*" *Cinema Papers,* November-December 1975, 264.

Novak, Glenn D., and Myles P. Breen. "Anti-Melodramatic Realism and Narrative Ambiguity in Peter Weir's *Picnic at Hanging Rock.*" *West Georgia College Review* 20 (1990): 1-14. A penetrating discussion on the film as possessing qualities of the typical melodramatic thriller and the art film, yet refusing to be categorized clearly as either.

Roginsky, Ed. "*Picnic at Hanging Rock.*" *Film Quarterly* 32, no. 4 (1979): 22-26. One of the most penetrating reviews of the film.

Wells, Jeffrey. "*Picnic at Hanging Rock.*" *Films in Review* 30, no. 5 (1979): 22.

The Last Wave

Boyd Russell. "Photographing *The Last Wave.*" *American Cinematographer* 59, no. 4 (1978): 352-55.

Clancy, Jack. "*The Last Wave.*" *Cinema Papers* 15 (1978): 259.

Combs, Richard. "*The Last Wave.*" *Sight and Sound* 47, no. 2 (1978): 121-22.

Gow, Gordon. "*The Last Wave.*" *Films and Filming* 24, no. 7 (1978): 34.

Mitchell, Robert. "*The Last Wave.*" In *Magill's Survey of Cinema,* edited by Frank N. Magill, 3:1325-29. Englewood Cliffs, N.Y.: Salem, 1981.

Pulleine, Tim. "*The Last Wave.*" *Monthly Film Bulletin* 45, no. 531 (1978): 66-67.

Routt, William D. "Are You a Fish? Are You a Snake?: An Obvious Lecture and Some Notes on *The Last Wave.*" *Continuum* 8, no. 2 (1994): 215-31.

An extensive discussion on several aspects of the film, containing many insights.

Zawojski, Piotr. "Świat jako projekcja świadomości: *Ostatnia fala*" (World as a Projection of Consciousness: *The Last Wave*). *Szwenk* 3 (1985): 11-21. Discusses the film in terms of its similarity to the literary world of "magic realism."

Gallipoli

Adams, Phillip. "*Gallipoli:* The Great Australian Love Story." *Age* (Australia), 22 August 1981, 24.

Beaver, Jim. "*Gallipoli.*" *Films in Review* 32, no. 8 (1981): 493-94.

Buchbinder, David. "Mateship, *Gallipoli,* and the Eternal Masculine." In *Representation, Discourse, and Desire: Contemporary Australian Culture and Critical Theory,* edited by Patrick Fuery, 115-37. London: Longman Cheshire, 1994. An important study that considers various readings of *Gallipoli* with respect to the wider issues of mateship.

Dobrez, Livio, and Pat. "Old Myths and New Delusions: Peter Weir's Australia." *Kunapipi* 4, no. 2 (1982): 61-75. An excellent study dealing with the film's representation of Australia and ideology.

Freebury, Jane. "Screening Australia—*Gallipoli:* A Study of Nationalism on Film." *Media Information Australia* 43 (1987): 5-8. Discusses the film's reception and its nationalist appeal.

Haltof, Marek. "In Quest of Self-Identity: *Gallipoli,* Mateship, and the Construction of Australian National Identity." *Journal of Popular Film and Television* 21, no. 1 (1993): 27-36. Discusses Weir's film as deeply rooted in the local mythology of Australia, as the endeavor to define the notion of the Australian nation.

Jaehne, Karen. "*Gallipoli.*" *Cineaste* 11, no. 4 (1982): 40-43.

Lawson, Sylvia. "*Gallipoli:* Picnic at the Pyramids." *Filmnews* 11/12 (1981): 11. A seminal review of the film pointing out its "conservative character."

Lohrey, Amanda. "Australian Mythologies: *Gallipoli:* Male Innocence as a Marketable Commodity." *Island* 9, no. 10 (1982): 29-34. A critical view of the film. Discusses the treatment of the myth of rural virtue as the most suspect and outdated in contemporary Australia.

McFarlane, Brian. "*Gallipoli.*" *Cinema Papers* 33 (1981): 20-21.

Pym, John. "*Gallipoli.*" *Monthly Film Bulletin* 48, no. 575 (1981): 244-45.

Rohdie, Sam. "*Gallipoli:* Peter Weir and an Australian Art Cinema." In *An Australian Film Reader,* edited by Albert Moran and Tom O'Regan, 194-97. Sydney: Currency, 1985.

———. "*Gallipoli* as World Camera Fodder." *Arena* 60 (1982): 36-42. Discusses the film's Australianess but notices its "international-commercial" formula.

Turner, Adrian. "*Gallipoli.*" *Films and Filming* 327 (1981): 33.

The Year of Living Dangerously

Durham, Carolyn A. "Visual Politics in *The Year of Living Dangerously:* To See or Not To See." *Perspectives on Contemporary Literature* 11 (1985): 117-25.

———. "*The Year of Living Dangerously:* Can Vision be a Model for Knowledge?" *Jump Cut* 30 (1985): 6-7. Focuses on Weir's "self-reflexive film in which the notion of the visual functions centrally as both image and theme."

Ehrlich, Linda C., and David Dungan, "*The Year of Living Dangerously:* An East-West Dialectic." *New Orleans Review* 19, no. 3-4 (1992): 118-24. An analysis of Weir's utilization of the Javanese puppet theater.

Elitzik, Paul. "*The Year of Living Dangerously.*" *Cineaste* 13, no. 2 (1984): 43-45.

Enker, Debi. "*The Year of Living Dangerously.*" *Cinema Papers* 42 (1983): 64-65.

MacBean, James Roy. "Watching the Third World Watchers." *Film Quarterly* 37, no. 3 (1984): 3-13. Provides a valuable discussion in the part subtitled "*The Year of Living Dangerously:* The Mysterious Orient, or Merely the Insensitive Western Observer?"

Roddick, Nick. "The Day of Living Dangerously: Indonesia Sept. 30, 1965." *Monthly Film Bulletin* 593 (1983): 148-49.

———. "*The Year of Living Dangerously.*" *Monthly Film Bulletin* 593 (1983): 147-48.

Spring, Lori. "The Other Dream: *The Year of Living Dangerously.*" *CineAction* 3/4 (1986): 58-71. An important academic article that employs psychoanalytic and Marxist approaches. It focuses on the film and dream analogy with reference to Weir's work as well as on the question of "otherness."

Witness

Bichard, Robert S. "*Witness*—John Seale ASC." *American Cinematographer* 4 (1986): 74-78.

Combs, Richard. "*Witness.*" *Monthly Film Bulletin* 52, no. 616 (1985): 166-67.

Hansen, Linda. "*Witness:* A New Image of Nonviolence in Popular Film." *Journal of Popular Film and Television* 14, no. 3 (1986): 136-41. Weir's film is considered in the broader cinematic context of American films dealing with images of nonviolent behavior.

Hostetter, Robert. "A Controversial *Witness.*" *Christian Century* 102 (1985): 341-42.

Kael, Pauline. "Plain and Simple: *Witness.*" *New Yorker,* 25 February 1985, 78-81.

Kauffmann, Stanley. "*Witness.*" *New Republic,* 22 December 1985, 24.

Kolker, Robert Phillip. "*Witness.*" *Cinema Papers* 51 (1985): 82-83.

McGowan, John P. "Looking at the (Alter)natives: Peter Weir's *Witness.*" *Chicago Review* 35, no. 3 (1986): 36-47. A major academic text analyzing the film from an anthropological perspective. *Witness* shows an alternative culture that exists as a functioning unit in the modern world.

Roddick, Nick. "Among the Amish." *Sight and Sound* 54, no. 3 (1985): 221-22.

Sragow, Michael. "Bearing Witness." *Film Comment* 21 (1985): 5-8.

The Mosquito Coast

Andrews, Terry L. "*The Mosquito Coast.*" In *Magill's Cinema Annual 1987: A Survey of the Films of 1986,* edited by Frank N. Magill, 307-13. Englewood Cliffs, N.J.: Salem, 1987.

Bawer, Bruce. "Life with Father." *American Spectator* 20, no. 2 (1987): 33-35.

Buckley, Michael. "*The Mosquito Coast.*" *Films in Review* 38, no. 2 (1987): 103-4.

Combs, Richard. "*The Mosquito Coast.*" *Monthly Film Bulletin* 54, no. 637 (1987): 52-53.

Connolly, Keith. "*The Mosquito Coast.*" *Cinema Papers* 61 (1987): 35.

Kauffmann, Stanley. "*The Mosquito Coast.*" *New Republic,* 22 December 1987, 26.

Lee, Nora. "*The Mosquito Coast:* A Jungle Utopia Gone Awry." *American Cinematographer* 68, no. 2 (1987): 60-65.

Rafferty, Terrence. "*The Mosquito Coast.*" *Nation* 243, no. 20 (1986), 683-84.

Dead Poets Society

Bawer, Bruce. "Poetry in Motion." *American Spectator* 22, no. 8 (August 1989): 39-40.

Carroll, John. "*Dead Poets Society* and Our Times." *Quadrant* 34, no. 3 (1990): 37-41. Discusses the film as pervaded by imagery of death. Many key ideas and insights.

Carton, Evan. "Better Dead Than Read: The Society of Poets." *Tikkun* 4, no. 6 (1989), 64-67. Provocative, critical essay on the film's ideology.

Combs, Richard. "*Dead Poets Society.*" *Monthly Film Bulletin* 6, no. 668 (1989): 272-73.

Delia, Mary, Alice. "*Dead Poets Society:* Uncritically Acclaimed." *Works and Days: Essays in the Socio-Historical Dimensions of Literature and the Arts* 9, no. 1 (1991): 91-96. Highly critical of the representation of the protagonist, whose "teaching practice contributes to his student's oppression rather than empowering them to learn and grow."

Geduld, Harry M. "Seize the Day?" *Humanist,* September/October 1989: 41-42.

Heilman, Robert B. "The Great-Teacher Myth." *American Scholar,* Summer 1989, 417-23. Illuminating discussion on the portrayal of Keating—not as a teacher but a performer, "a fraud as a hero." Lively comments with reference to Keatings in contemporary world of education.

Kael, Pauline. "Stonework." *New Yorker,* 26 June 1989, 70-71.

Kauffmann, Stanley. "Boys' Lives." *New Republic,* 26 June 1989, 28-29.

Luby, Barbra. "*Dead Poets Society.*" *Filmnews* 19, no. 6 (1989): 12-13.

McFarlane, Brian. "*Dead Poets Society.*" *Cinema Papers* 75 (1989): 52-53.

Rooks, Pamela R. "Woo Who? Exclusion of Otherness in *Dead Poets Society.*" *Australian Journal of Communication* 18, no. 2 (1991): 75-83. Argues that the film is an unfortunate triumph of style over substance.

Simon, John. "The Red, Red Robin Comes Blabbin' Along." *National Review,* 15 September 1989, 54-55.

Spitz, Ellen Handler. "Carpe Diem, Carpe Mortam: Reflections on *Dead Poets Society.*" *Post Script: Essays in Film and the Humanities* 11, no. 3 (1992): 19-31. An insightful, lengthy article that focuses on the forms and messages of American popular culture as presented in Weir's film.

Green Card

Glaessner, Verina. "*Green Card.*" *Monthly Film Bulletin* 58, no. 586 (1991): 79-80.

Hearty, Kitty Bowe. "French Connection." *Premiere* 4, no. 6 (1991): 59-62

Jacka, Liz. "*Green Card.*" *Filmnews* 21, no. 1 (1991): 14.

Mayer, Geoff. "*Green Card.*" *Cinema Papers* 82 (1991): 53-54.

Fearless

Fisher, Bob. "*Fearless* Explores Emotional Aftermath of Fateful Flight." *American Cinematographer* 74, no. 11 (1993): 40-51.

Luby, Barbra. "*Fearless.*" *Filmnews* 23, no. 5 (1994): 12-13.

Murray, Scott. "*Fearless.*" *Cinema Papers* 100 (1994): 67-68.

Rafferty, Terrence. "After the Crash." *New Yorker,* 25 October 1993, 120-22.

Simon, John. "Believe It Who Will." *National Review,* 29 November 1993, 69-71.

FILMOGRAPHY

Count Vim's Last Exercise (1967)
(15 minutes, 16mm, black and white)

The Life and Flight of the Rev. Buck Shotte (1968)
(33 minutes, 16mm, black and white)

Michael (episode in *Three to Go*) (1970)
(31 minutes, 16mm, black and white)
Production company: Commonwealth Film Unit
Producer: Gil Brealey
Assistant director: Brian Hannant
Screenplay: Peter Weir
Photography: Kerry Brown
Editing: Wayne Le Clos
Music: The Cleves
Cast: Matthew Burton (Michael), Grahame Bond (Grahame), Peter Colville
      (Neville Trantor), Georgina West (Georgina), Betty Lucas (Mother), Judy
      McBurney (Judy)

Stirring the Pool (1970)
(6 minutes, documentary, 16mm, color)

Homesdale (1971)
(52 minutes, fiction, 16mm, black and white)
Production company: Experimental Film Fund
Producers: Richard Brennan, Grahame Bond
Assistant director: Brian Hannant
Screenplay: Peter Weir, Piers Davies
Photography: Anthony Wallis
Editing: Wayne Le Clos
Music: Grahame Bond, Rory O'Donoghue
Cast: Geoff Malone (Mr. Malfrey), Grahame Bond (Kevin), Kate Fitzpatrick
      (Miss Greenoak), James Dellit (Manager), Kosta Akon (Chief Robert),
      Richard Brennam (Robert 1), Peter Weir (Robert 2), Phil Noyce

(Neville), Shirley Donald (Matron), James Lear (Mr. Levy), Barry Donelly (Mr. Vaughn)

Australian Colour Diary No. 43: Three Directions in Australian Pop Music (1972)

(10 minutes, documentary, 16mm, color)
Production company: ACFU
Producer: Malcolm Otton
Photography: Michael Edols
Editing: Jim Coffey
Sound: Julian Ellingworth

Boat Building (1972)

(4 minutes, color)

The Billiond Room (1972)

(6 minutes, color)

The Computer Centre (1972)

(5 minutes, color)

The Field Day (1972)

(5 minutes, color)

Tempo: Australia in the 70s (1972)

(24 minutes, color, script only; director, Keith Gow)

Incredible Floridas (1972)

(12 minutes, documentary, 35mm, color)
Production company: Film Australia
Producer: Malcolm Otton
Screenplay: Peter Weir
Photography: Bruce Hillyard
Editing: Anthony Buckley
Music: Richard Meale

Whatever Happened to Green Valley (1973)

(55 minutes, documentary, 16mm, color)
Production company: Film Australia
Producer: Anthony Buckley
Screenplay: Peter Weir
Photography: Nick Ardizzone, Don McAlpine, Ross King, Guy Furner
Editing: Barry Williams

The Fifth Facade (1973)

(documentary)
Director: Donald Crombie
Screenplay: Peter Weir, Keith Gow, Donald Crombie

The Cars That Ate Paris (1974)

(91 minutes, feature, color)
Production company: Salt Pan Films and Royce Smeal Productions
Producers: Jim McElroy, Hal McElroy
Assistant director: Hal McElroy
Screenplay: Peter Weir, Keith Gow, Piers Davies; based on a story by Peter
    Weir
Cinematography: John McLean
Camera operators: Richard Wallis, Peter James
Editing: Wayne Le Clos
Art director: David Copping
Music: Bruce Smeaton
Sound recording: Hen Hammond
Sound mixing: Peter Fenton
Stunt coordination: Ken Hammond
Cast: Terry Camilleri (Arthur Waldo), John Meillon (Mayor), Kevin Miles
    (Dr. Midland), Melissa Jaffer (Beth), Max Gillies (Metcalf), Danny
    Adcock (Policeman), Bruce Spence (Charlie), Rick Scully (George),
    Max Phipps (Rev. Mulray), Peter Armstrong (Gorman), Chris Haywood
    (Daryl), Deryck Barnes (Al Smedley), Charles Metcalfe (Clive Smedley),
    Joe Burrow (Ganger), Edward Howell (Tringham), Tim Robertson
    (Les), Herbie Nelson (Man in House), Kevin Golsby (Insurance Man)

Fugue (1974)

(short, writer only)

Picnic at Hanging Rock (1975)

(115 minutes, feature, color)
Production company: Picnic Productions, in association with BEF Film Dis-
    tributors, SAFCO, AFC
Producers: Hal McElroy and Jim McElroy with Patricia Lovell
Assistant directors: Mark Egerton, Kim Dalton, Ian Jamieson
Screenplay: Cliff Green; based on the novel *Picnic at Hanging Rock* by Joan
    Lindsay
Cinematography: Russell Boyd
Camera operator: John Seale
Nature photography: David Sanderson
Editing: Max Lemon

Art director: David Copping
Music: Bruce Smeaton, "Pan Pipe" by Gheorghe Zamphir
Costumes: Judy Dorsman
Costume consultant: Wendy Weir
Art adviser: Martin Sharp
Sound editing: Greg Bell
Sound recording: Don Connelly
Cast: Rachel Roberts (Mrs. Appleyard), Dominic Guard (Michael Fitzhubert), Anne Lambert (Miranda), Karen Robson (Irma), Margaret Nelson (Sara), Helen Morse (Diane de Poitiers), Vivean Gray (Miss McCraw), John Jarratt (Albert), Kirsty Child (Miss Lumley), Jane Vallis (Marion), Christine Schuler (Edith), Jacki Weaver (Minnie), Anthony Llewellyn-Jones (Tom), Frank Gunnell (Mr. Whitehead), John Fegan (Dr. McKenzie), Wyn Roberts (Sergeant Bumpher), Ingrid Mason (Rosamund), Peter Colingwood (Col. Fitzhubert), Olga Dickie (Mrs. Fitzhubert), Faith Kleinig (Cook), Jenny Lovell (Blanche), Janet Murray (Juliana), Martin Vaughan (Ben Hussey), Jack Fegan (Doc McKenzie), Garry McDonald (Jim Jones), Kay Taylor (Mrs. Bumpher), Vivienne Graves, Angela Bencini, Melinda Cardwell, Annabel Powrie, Amanda White, Lindy O'Connell, Verity Smith, Deborah Mullins, Sue Jamieson, Bernadette Bencini, Barbara Lloyd

Three Workshop Films (1975)
(28 minutes, color)
Directors: Peter Weir, Don Crombie, Peter Maxwell
Production company: The Film and Television School, Sydney
Producer: John Morris
Screenplay: Vince O'Donnell, Grant Reed
Photography: Milton B. Ingerson
Editing: Bob Allen

Luke's Kingdom (1977)
(TV series, two episodes)

The Last Wave (1977)
(106 minutes, feature, color)
Production company: Ayer Productions, A McElroy and McElroy Production in association with Derek Power, SAFCO, AFC
Producers: Hal McElroy, Jim McElroy
Assistant director: John Robertson, Ian Jamieson
Screenplay: Peter Weir, Tony Morphett, Petru Popescu; based an original idea by Peter Weir
Cinematography: Russell Boyd

Camera operator: John Seale
Additional photography: Ron Taylor, George Greenough, Klaus Jaritz
Art director: Neil Angwin
Editing: Max Lemon
Music: Charles Wain
Sound recording: Don Connolly
Sound mixer: Greg Bell
Special effects: Monty Fieguth, Robert Hilditch
Production design: Goran Warff
Adviser on Aboriginal matters: Lance Bennett
Cast: Richard Chamberlain (David Burton), Olivia Hamnett (Annie Burton), David Gulpilil (Chris Lee), Nandjiwarra Amagula (Charlie), Frederick Parslow (Reverend Burton), Vivean Gray (Dr. Whitburn), Walter Amagula (Gerry Lee), Roy Bara (Larry), Cedric Lalara (Lindsey), Morris Lalara (Jacko), Athol Compton (Billy Corman), Hedley Cullen (Judge), Peter Carroll (Michael Zaedler), Michael Duffield (Andrew Potter), Wallas Eaton (Morgue Doctor), Jo England (Babysitter), John Frawley (Policeman), Jennifer de Greenlaw (Zeadler's Secretary), Richard Henderson (Prosecutor), Penny Leach (Schoolteacher), Merv Lilley, John Meagher, Guido Rametta, Malcolm Robertson, Greg Rowe

The Plumber (1978)

(76 minutes, TV feature, color)
Production company: South Australian Film Corporation
Producer: Matt Carroll
Screenplay: Peter Weir
Cinematography: David Sanderson
Camera operator: Peter Moss
Art directors: Herbert Pinter, Ken James
Editing: Gerald Turney-Smith
Music: Rory O'Donohue
Sound: Ken Hammond
Production designer: Wendy Weir
Cast: Judy Morris (Jill Cowper), Ivar Kants (Max the Plumber), Robert Coleby (Brian Cowper), Candy Raymond (Meg), Henri Szeps (Department Head), Yiomi Abiodun, Beverley Roberts, Bruce Rosen, Daphne Grey

Heart and Hand: Peter Rushforth, Potter (1979)

(25 minutes, documentary, color with black and white sequences)
Production company: Crafts Council of Australia
Photography: John Seale
Editing: Bob Cogger
Sound: Don Connolly

Gallipoli (1981)

(111 minutes, feature, color)
Production company: Associated R and R Films
Executive producer: Francis O'Brien
Producer: Robert Stigwood, Patricia Lovell
Assistant producers: Martin Cooper, Ben Gannon
Assistant directors: Mark Egerton, Steve Andrews, Marshall Crosby, Robert
    Pendlebury; Egypt, Attef El Taieb
Screenplay: David Williamson; based on a story by Peter Weir
Cinematography: Russell Boyd
Camera operator: John Seale
Underwater photography: Ron Taylor
Editing: William Anderson
Music: Brian May
Sound recording: Don Connolly
Design coordinator: Wendy Weir
Special effects: Chris Murray, Monty Fieguth, David Hardie, Steve Courtley,
    Bruce Henderson
Military adviser: Bill Gammage
Cast: Mark Lee (Archy Hamilton), Mel Gibson (Frank Dunne), Bill Hunter
    (Major Barton), Tim McKenzie (Barney Wilson), David Argue
    ("Snowy"), Robert Grubb (Billy), Bill Kerr (Uncle Jack), Harold
    Baigent (Stumpy), Ron Graham (Wallace Hamilton), Charles
    Yunupingu (Zac), Harold Hopkins (Les McCann), Heath Harris (Stock-
    man), Gerda Nicolson (Rose Hamilton), Brian Anderson (Angus), Reg
    Evans (1st official), Jack Giddy (2d official), Dane Peterson (Announcer),
    Paul Linkson (Recruiting Officer), Jenny Lovell (Waitress), Steve Dodd
    (Billy Lionel), Phyllis Burford (Laura), Marjorie Irving (Gran), John
    Murphy (Dan Dunne), Peter Ford (Lt. Gray), Diane Chamberlain (Anne
    Barton), Ian Govett (Army Doctor), Geoff Parry (Sgt. Sayers), Clive
    Bennington (1st English Officer), Giles Holland-Martin (2d English
    Officer), Moshe Kedem (Egyptian Shopkeeper), John Morris (Colonel
    Robinson), Paul Sonkkila (Sniper)

Man of the Earth (1980)

(30 minutes, documentary, color)
Director and screenwriter: P. Butt
Editors: Peter Weir, Robert Coggen

The Year of Living Dangerously (1982)

(115 minutes, feature, color)
Production company: A McElroy and McElroy Production, A Freddie Fields
    presentation, for MGM/UA with development assistance from the Aus-
    tralian Film Commission

Producer: Jim McElroy

Assistant directors: Mark Egerton, Chris Webb, Michael Bourchier; Phillip-
ines crew, Wayne Barry, Ulysses Formanez, Ken Richardson, Robert
Woolcott, Jose Angeles

Screenplay: David Williamson, Peter Weir, C. J. Koch; based on the C. J. Koch
novel *The Year of Living Dangerously*

Cinematography: Russell Boyd

Second unit photography: John Seale

Camera operator: Nixon Binney

Editing: William Anderson

Music: Maurice Jarre

Design coordinator: Wendy Weir

Costume design: Terry Ryan

Special effects: Danny Dominguez

Cast: Mel Gibson (Guy Hamilton), Sigourney Weaver (Jill Bryant), Linda
Hunt (Billy Kwan), Michael Murphy (Pete Curtis), Bembol Roco
(Kumar), Noel Ferrier (Wally O'Sullivan), Bill Kerr (Col. Henderson),
Paul Sonkkila (Kevin Condon), Kuh Ledesman (Tiger Lily), Cecily Pol-
son (Moira), Domingo Landicho (Hortono), Hermino de Guzman
(Immigration Officer), Ali Nur (Ali), Dominador Robridillo (Betjak
Man), Mike Emperio (President Sukarno), Bernardo Nacilla (Dwarf),
Coco Marantha (Pool Waiter), David Oyang (Hadji), Lito Tolentino
(Udin), Mark Egerton (Embassy Aid), Norma Uatuhan (Ipu)

Witness (1985)

(112 minutes, feature, color)

Production company: Paramount Pictures Corporation

Producer: Edward S. Feldman

Coproduction: David Bombyk

Associate producer: Wendy Weir

Assistant directors: David McGiffert, Pamela Eilerson

Screenplay: Earl W. Wallace, William Kelley; from a story by William Kelley,
Pamela Wallace, Earl Wallace

Photography: John Seale

Camera operator: Dan Lerner

Editing: Thom Noble

Music: Maurice Jarre

Production design: Stan Jolley

Special effects: John R. Elliott

Amish adviser: John D. King

Cast: Harrison Ford (John Book), Kelly McGillis (Rachel Lapp), Lukas Haas
(Samuel Lapp), Josef Sommer (Schaeffer), Jan Rubes (Eli Lapp), Alexander Godunov (Daniel Hochleitner), Danny Glover (McFee), Brent Jen-
nings (Carter), Angus McInnes (Fergie), Patti LuPone (Elaine), Frederick

Rolf (Stoltzfus), Viggo Mortensen (Moses Hochleitner), Ed Crowley (Scheriff), John Garson (Bishop Tchantz), Beverly May (Mrs. Yoder), Timothy Carhart (Zenovich), Sylvia Kauders (Tourist Lady), Marian Swan (Mrs. Schaeffer)

The Mosquito Coast (1986)

(119 minutes, feature, color)
Production company: The Saul Zaentz Co.
Executive producer: Saul Zaentz
Producer: Jerome Hellman
Associative producer: Neville Thompson
Assistant directors: Mark Egerton, Steve Andrews, Philip Patterson, Russ Kneeland
Screenplay: Paul Schrader; based on the novel *The Mosquito Coast* by Paul Theroux
Cinematography: John Seale
Editing: Thom Noble
Music: Maurice Jarre
Sound recording: Chris Newman
Sound effects: Ann Kroeber
Production design: John Stoddart
Special effects: Larry Cavanaugh (coordinator), Bruce Steinheimer (supervisor), Joe Lombardi (consultant)
Cast: Harrison Ford (Allie Fox), Helen Mirren (Mother), River Phoenix (Charlie Fox), Jadrien Steele (Jerry Fox), Hilary Gordon (April Fox), Rebecca Gordon (Clover Fox), Dick O'Neill (Mr. Polski), André Gregory (Rev. Spellgood), Alice Sneed (Mrs. Polski), Tiger Haynes (Mr. Semper), Conrad Roberts (Mr. Hardy), Melanie Boland (Mrs. Spellgood), Martha Plimpton (Emily Spellgood), Jason Alexander (Clerk), William Newman (Captain Smalls), Michael Roberts (Francis Lungley), Tony Vega (Mr. Maywit), Aurora Clavel (Mrs. Maywit), Butterfly McQueen (Ma Kennywick)

Dead Poets Society (1989)

(129 minutes, feature, color)
Production company: Touchstone Pictures in association with Silver Screen Partners IV
Producers: Steven Haft, Paul Junger Witt, Tony Thomas
Assistant directors: Alan B. Curtis, B. Thomas Seidman
Screenplay: Tom Schulman
Cinematography: John Seale
Camera operator: Stephen Shank
Editing: William Anderson
Music: Maurice Jarre

Production design: Wendy Stites
Cast: Robin Williams (John Keating), Robert Sean Leonard (Neil Perry), Ethan Hawke (Todd Anderson), Josh Charles (Knox Overstreet), Gale Hansen (Charlie Dalton), Dylan Kussman (Richard Cameron), Allelon Ruggiero (Steven Meeks), James Waterston (Gerald Pitts), Norman Lloyd (Mr. Nolan), Kurtwood Smith (Mr. Perry), Carla Belver (Mrs. Perry), Leon Pownall (McAllister), George Martin (Dr. Hager), Joe Aufiery (Chemistry Teacher), Matt Carey (Hopkins), Kevin Cooney (Joe Danburry), Jane Morre (Mrs. Danburry), Lara Flynn Boyle (Ginny Danburry), Colin Irving (Chet Danburry), Alexandra Powers (Chris Noel), Melora Walters (Gloria), Welker White (Tina), Steve Mathios (Steve), John Cunningham (Mr. Anderson), Debra Mooney (Mrs. Anderson)

Green Card (1990)

(108 minutes, feature, color)
Production company: Touchstone Pictures
Executive producer: Edward S. Feldman
Producer: Peter Weir
Assistant directors: Alan B. Curtis, Liz Ryan
Cinematography: Geoffrey Simpson
Camera operator: Ken Ferris
Music: Hans Zimmer
Editing: William Anderson
Production design: Wendy Stites
Cast: Gérard Depardieu (Georges Faure), Andie MacDowell (Brontë Parrish), Bebe Neuwirth (Lauren), Gregg Edelman (Phil), Robert Prosky (Brontë's Lawyer), Jessie Keosian (Mrs. Bird), Ethan Phillips (Gorsky), Mary Louise Wilson (Mrs. Sheehan), Lois Smith, Conrad McLaren (Brontë's Parents)

Fearless (1993)

(119 minutes, feature, color)
Production company: A Spring Creek Production, distributed by Warner Bros.
Producers: Paula Weinstein, Mark Rosenberg
Assistant directors: John Rusk
Screenplay: Rafael Yglesias; based on his novel Fearless
Cinematography: Allen Daviau
Camera operator: Paul C. Babin
Editing: William Anderson
Music: Maurice Jarre
Production design: John Stoddart
Special design consultant: Wendy Stites
Special effects coordinator: Ken Pepiot

Cast: Jeff Bridges (Max Klein), Isabella Rossellini (Laura Klein), Rosie Perez (Carla Rodrigo), Tom Hulce (Brillstein), Dr. Bill Perlman (John Turturro), Benicio Del Toro (Manny Rodrigo), Deirdre O'Connell (Nan Gordon), John de Lancie (Jeff Gordon), Spencer Vrooman (Jonah Klein), Robin Pearson Rose (Sarah), Debra Monk (Alison), Cynthia Mace (Cindy Dickens), Randle Mell (Peter Hummel), Kathryn Rossetter (Jennifer Hummel), Craig Rovere, Doug Ballard (FBI Agents)

INDEX

THE AUTHOR

Marek Haltof is a film critic and writer working at the University of
Western Ontario in London, Canada. He was born in Cieszyn,
Poland, and is a graduate of the University of Silesia (Poland),
Flinders University of South Australia, and the University of Alberta,
Canada (Ph.D.).

His articles on popular culture and on Australian and Polish cinema have appeared in such journals as *Kino, Film Quarterly, S—European Journal for Semiotic Studies, Journal of Popular Film and Television*,
and *Canadian Slavonic Papers*. He is the author of a collection of essays
on American popular cinema, *Kino lęków* (The Cinema of Fears), a
book on Australian New Wave Cinema, *Kino Australii: O ekranowej
konstrukcji Australii* (Australian Cinema: On the Screen Construction
of Australia), and two novels, *Maks jest wielki* (Max Is Great) and *Duo
Nowak*, all published in Poland.

THE EDITOR

Frank E. Beaver, General Editor of Twayne's Filmmakers Series, was born in Cleveland, North Carolina, in 1938. He was educated at the University of North Carolina, Chapel Hill (B.A., M.A.), and at the University of Michigan (Ph.D.), where he chairs the Department of Communication. He has authored three books on the art and history of the motion picture as well as *Oliver Stone: Wakeup Cinema* (1993) and the *Dictionary of Film Terms* (1994), both published in Twayne's Filmmakers Series. For twenty years he has served as media commentator for National Public Radio stations WUOM-WVGR-WFUM.

Please
return
materials
on time